Trade the OEX

Trade
the OEX
Cut Risk
Not Profit
Third Edition

Arthur Darack

Bonus Books, Inc., Chicago

99   98   97   96   95   5   4   3   2   1

Library of Congress Cataloging-in-Publication Data

Darack, Arthur.
    Trade the OEX : cut risk, not profit / Arthur Darack.—3rd ed.
        p.   cm.
    Includes index.
    ISBN 1-56625-032-3 (cloth)
    1. Stock index futures.   I. Title.
    HG6043.D39   1995
    332.63′228—dc20   95-6435
                                                           CIP

Bonus Books, Inc.
160 East Illinois Street
Chicago, Illinois 60611

Printed in the United States of America

Contents

Preface

Everybody knows that there is a world market, for ideas and goods, for investments and plunder. As populations explode, the world's resources wear thin, except in the theories of some professors who never leave their lecture halls and so cannot see the squalor that has overtaken many areas of the globe where once some form of tribal prosperity was enjoyed. Is Wall St. such an area? Not for followers of the OEX.

In recent years, as Wall St. becomes more automated and more internationalized, and a toy of computer programs wielded by the new style gunslinger (read "fund manager"), it appears to be taking on pallor. While they still clean the streets in the area, much has been plundered. Downsizing, restructuring and other forms of terrorism have been the much applauded order of the day. When you chop a company or industry down to size, the stock usually goes up in anticipation of higher profitability, or full profitability ahead and damn the employees. It doesn't always work out that way. Profitability is under pressure from world competition in every field. Wall St. is no exception. Thousands of financial experts have been retired by automation and other forms of displacement. Perhaps they will be retrained as politicians. The turmoil and unease in financial markets accompany world upset since the fall of communism. Every former communist state and every emerging or Third World state set up rickety stock markets in hopes of achieving wealth quickly. Everybody wants the fast buck.

Does this mean that the markets themselves are not to be trusted with your rent money? The major stock markets are as safe as sin—no danger of imploding or departing. But they behave differently these days.

With the market trading around 4000 (Dow), instead of around 2000, as it was when we first addressed the OEX, there are several other changed features that must be pondered. A 10% swing in a 4000 Dow market is 400 points compared to only 200 in a Dow of 2000. But one OEX point usually equals about 7 Dow points, so it takes about 100 points in the Dow to force a move of 14 OEX points. It follows that spreads need to be wider. The relationship between 1 OEX point to 7 Dow points has not changed, but the higher market means greater swings—more volatility, more menace to spreads chosen for richness of premium, not for width of spread, i.e., safety.

You need to hedge more carefully, selecting spreads of larger intervals than in the past. Inevitably, that means premiums will be smaller. THAT means you should increase the number of contracts, from 5 to 10 or 20 or more. Each contract requires a margin, thus doubling, quadrupling, etc., the amount of margin capital you need to employ. That money, of course, is yours, deposited with the broker in case the trade goes against you. Stocks and bonds qualify as margin. But losses in vertical spreading can always be kept to a few hundred dollars in a 10-contract spread, or rarely more than $1,000 in a 20-contract effort.

Does all this mean the party's over? No. A Paul Revere style rescue has saved the day in the shape of collars. Those NYSE collars that were installed after the crash of 1987 keep market swings under control when the Dow reaches 50 points up or down. That stops program trading, the usual source of high volatility. Markets rarely get beyond 50 or 60 without program trading. So the OEX cause is not lost, merely altered a bit.

Introduction

Markets change because of changes in what they represent. Stocks, bonds, options and money all change in value, in how they are perceived and manipulated, because society changes. Work, the basis of all wealth, has been changing fundamentally since the advent of the computer. But work has always been changing fundamentally, since the discovery of fire and the advent of the wheel. Today it changes more rapidly because the computer speeds everything up.

Fire also speeds everything up, but it destroys in the process if it is uncontrolled. Perhaps the computer is not unlike the fire. We see the computer at work in every cranny of society, speeding up the replacement of one activity with another. One of the most difficult of all changes to accept is the most fundamental—work. In Third World countries few changes in work have occurred. In all industrialized societies a person over 65 would not be able to work in an office that had been computerized since that person left. It is not surprising that all work has changed, since the supermarkets you shop in, the car you drive, the house you leave to go shopping, the gas station you frequent, the traffic light that annoys you and the concert ticket you purchase, have all changed because of the computer. Every industrial and commercial process has changed thanks to the computer. Has your thinking about all these things changed correspondingly?

In order to survive in such a world you had better be able to answer "yes."

For reasons of this sort you need to think hard about

money. It too has changed, along with work. One thing to do
with about 5% of your money is to look at OEX options.

Options have become a dirty word; they are "derivatives."
Now, if you said it, go wash your mouth with soap, if you
are a true believer in the latest cant, that the production of
wealth is a sin. Hillary Rodham Clinton assailed the pharma-
ceutical industry for its profitability until it was discovered that
she thought nothing of speculating in cattle futures to the tune
of turning $1,000 into $100,000. Strictly speaking, futures are
not derivatives, but they are close enough. If the CEO of Merck
or Pfizer were to be caught using company funds to trade
cattle futures, they would be pilloried (Hillaried?), and
rightly so. Mrs. Clinton used her own money to some extent,
but the trade, as described in the papers, could not have
occurred for a multitude of reasons unless it was actually done
by a professional "sitting in" for the then Governor Clinton's
wife. Financial officers of large companies may use all manner
of investments but typically they do not trade cattle futures,
which are as risky as the futures recommended in this book
(S&P 500) and certainly ruinous to anyone who hasn't done it
repeatedly after the most careful study. So what are derivatives
and why are they dirty words?

The Clinton Administration came to power promising to
get the rest of the country even with all those who profited in
the Reagan and Bush administrations. That included every
profitable company in the land, apparently, and anyone who
made more than the typical member of the middle class, which
could be anyone making over $30,000, one judges. A cynic
from Mars would be led to think that profitability is a sin;
making money is wicked. But it is the absence of money that
causes more human misery than anything except war and
revolution. The fall of communism demonstrated to everyone,
except those closet Marxists in and out of government who are
true believers, that there can be no good society for anyone

outside the ruling class unless there is profitability for everyone. Only capitalism can make profit for everyone a possibility, a fact that Mrs. Clinton admits when she uses her own money but not where everyone else's is concerned. The OEX and other "derivatives" were children of the '80s, though trading devices based on more fundamental mechanisms are as natural as trading baseball cards for chewing gum (or pennies), and only became notorious since the Clintons came to Washington and declared wealth (other than their own) to be wicked.

Some uses of derivatives were indeed stupid, foolish and disastrous to users unaware of their volatilities and dangers. All options, and especially the OEX Index, have always been risky in the hands of the reckless. But all life involves risk, almost every step of the way. It ill behooves an administration that has seen a mad surge in the proliferation of gambling throughout the land, in casinos, gambling boats, and slot machines everywhere you walk, to say nothing of the state lotteries which had nothing to do with the Clintons, to look askance at the risks of derivative financial instruments.

Next there will be congressional investigations of baseball cards, which are derivative financial instruments as noted above. The fact is that while most gambling enriches only the owners of the slot machines (and the gangsters, and the essential employees), traders in options and other derivative financial instruments send money into the U.S. financial structure. The product of every options trade ought to be a contribution to somebody's wealth; the effects of gambling, except to the owners, are mostly a highly regressive tax on a disastrous impulse—to gamble recklessly. OEX options are a gamble, as is every use of money in an investing or speculating situation. But anyone who acquires the necessary skills and information can learn to use options as an investing situation where risks occur that are not unlike those of pulling on slot machine levers. How? Why?

No matter how much caution you exercise in dealing with financial markets, you are always at risk. Nobody can predict such an event as the stock market crash October 19, 1987, when the market dropped over 22 percent in one day—a bear market, if you please, compressed within eight hours. Many conservative investors "took a bath" on that day. (Cleanliness in this case is not next to godliness.)

But that is a once-in-a-lifetime event.

You can, to be sure, pull on slot machine levers cautiously, and some people do win—a few hundred dollars here and there, sometimes a lot more. But a typical gambler loses far more often than he wins, whereas the reverse is true with investors.

I said that the end product of gambling contributes little or nothing to economic growth and well-being, especially to those who lose their money—the vast majority. But, of course, many gambling resorts trade on exchanges, and many restaurants and nearby service professionals are supported in part by gambling patrons. If gambling is your only recreation, and you lose money that you can't replace or afford, gambling becomes a menace. Investing, even when it involves higher levels of risk, pushes money into the foundations of economic growth, especially yours.

The most pervasive enemy of economic growth is not gambling but government regulation and taxes. The Bush Administration, supposedly pro-business, was not much better than Clinton in the strapping of business with onerous regulation and taxes. Government regulations proliferated under Bush like weeds in Florida. Bureaucratic interference in the economy wasn't invented by Clinton (or Bush); it won't go away with Clinton's departure. But it is well to remember that Clinton's appeal to the class struggle of Marxism—tax the rich because they made out like bandits in the '80s—was a shabby electoral device that worked politically. Capitalism works because people with money invest it and people with the most money invest the most. When you take the most money away from the people who have the most, you penalize the economy; the rich don't suffer, particularly. The idea of class warfare led to history's vilest century of mass murder and revolution; the themes of Stalin and Hitler. One should not look charitably upon politicians who invoke such ghosts, or academics who find tortured "reasons" to support these apparitions.

None of this is to be interpreted as an argument that derivative instruments of speculation on Wall St. will save the world. They will do nothing of the sort. If you do it right they will make you rich or at least better off financially than when you gamble or work at a low-paying, uncertain task. But that's true of all investing in U.S. markets and indeed is truer by far in the case of stocks and bonds. These are the truest source of wealth through investments (along with real estate at the right time and place). Options are icing on cakes.

Before we conclude that options are the main villain in the derivatives debate in the U.S. Congress, Wall St. and elsewhere, it may be noted that the offending instruments were not options at all; they were such things as leveraged swaps, structured notes and other arcana. In fact, options were insufficiently risky, hence profitable, for most fund managers needing high performance—higher than government paper, for example. Options are hedging instruments par excellence, among other things, and hedges limit both profit and risk. Nobody is proposing to regulate options—yet. But Congress gets spasms periodically about the financial markets, which it does not understand. So it gets defensive, ruinous and in its regulating-vindictive mood.

Everyone ought to understand something of derivatives, not that they are like AIDS or high-fat diet. But they are all around us, like criminals and crazy ideas, only they are neither. The derivatives market can make your head swim in its size and complexity. Derivatives are as old as sin but not yet the stuff of soap or grand operas. Baseball cards are an example. In themselves they have only sentimental value, but they derive real value from the multi-billion dollar game itself, the stars and their performance. These are underlying assets. All derivatives are of value because of what they represent. The underlying value of derivatives is about $35 trillion, which is almost three-fourths of all the stocks and bonds in the world. Stocks and bonds (and mutual funds, money market accounts and bank accounts) are also derivatives in the sense that they represent something else, i.e., derived from something else— values in expressed monetary units based on governments, corporations and other organizations that will redeem them at face value or values published on a daily basis. Derivatives take this representation one step further; they are based on stocks and bonds and their daily changes in value. So, in Plato's words, they are one further step removed from reality, and the present anger over them and their risk has some good old Platonic condemnation in it. The reality they represent is the world's wealth-producing industry, commerce, business and art. Derivatives are not themselves wealth-producing; they are speculations on the wealth and financial instruments that represent wealth. Thus they are among the earliest symbols of wealth. In an age when wealth is despised in theory but not in practice, derivatives better watch out.

All wealth is based on work, i.e., labor which has both real and speculative value, on machines, on an endless list of products most of which are made by machines nowadays, and by every conceivable kind of intellectual activity, including the production of books, movies, ballets and symphonies, canvases and television. All originate partly in some kind of speculative activity, in some kind of planning, fantasy, organization and strategy. When someone asks how much you charge to perform a certain task, you say "I'll have to figure it out and give you an estimate." Much of the figuring is speculation—on how long it will take, on what the competition will charge, etc. Financial speculation isn't quite like that but it is based on a study of many features of the environment it entails and the competition for your dollar and attention. If the use of options won't get you where you want to go, financially, you will spend the money on something else.

All markets, including options, are based on the search for prices and values. The progress of most markets goes from turbulence to crisis to panic, despite the ultimate goal of market participants, which is stability. Simple souls seeking relief from worry trust in banks, money market funds, and government paper. Banks and money market funds pay short term interest rates, which usually aren't much higher than inflation (3.3 percent at the moment). Government notes and bonds are the backbone of a lot of cautious investor portfolios, especially retirement plans. But stocks pay a lot more over time and so do bonds when interest rates aren't driving them into the ground, as during the second year of the Clinton Administration. Stocks, bonds and mutual funds (based on equities) should comprise about 90 percent of your investment dollars. The rest should be in cash and options, if you have the time and talent for it, to say nothing of the right psychology.

Financial markets now are worldwide, dominated by the huge fund managers, mutual funds like Fidelity and Vanguard and the big pension funds. Increasingly, world markets follow dutifully along the path of U.S. markets. That is because the U.S. is the world's chief economic engine, followed distantly by Japan and Western Europe. Russia and China will become big players over time, once they clear away the detritus of the Marxist madness, as will India, not so far gone into Marxism. Without U.S. markets Japan would still be a third world country scrounging for capital and markets. We handed over the most lucrative market in the world (ours) and made them a super financial power. Their own genius made them a super industrial power, but their response to us has hardly been gracious.

Few financial planners allot any portion of income to our subject, the OEX, yet the OEX can be used in high and low risk situations, differing little from stocks and bonds in these respects, especially growth stocks and junk bonds. When you buy stocks for the long haul you always risk big market swings. If you depend on market timing to get you in and out of the market at the best time, you will end up making your broker rich; you will end up wiser and poorer. Knowing when to sell a stock remains one of life's mysteries, unless you have a hard and fast rule. Options can hedge against big market swings and make money in the process.

Is market timing fraudulent? Everyone uses some form of it, and we are no exception, as you will see. But we don't depend on it. Markets give off signals constantly, in response to their major players. Some insight into what moves markets can be found each day in the *Wall Street Journal* and in the daily stream of information on the Financial News Network. But our purposes are best served in markets that move very little, or move back and forth over a trading range. So, we don't hitch our wagon to the stars of market timing.

But the OEX can be especially useful in markets that move violently, as we will see. Highly volatile markets come along often without warning and disappear just as suddenly. Options can be useful in such markets.

Learning about options needs both theoretical and practical information and skill. You can start with a book but you will need to practice for several months at least before taking the plunge. Two or three months of practice should be a kind of spring training for the long season ahead. You cannot win at options or investing in stocks and bonds unless you know what you are doing (or have a broker who is absolutely trustworthy).

In dealing with markets you face a daunting statistical array. One should not be intimidated by statistics. Many great economists, from Friedman to Keynes, have played down the role of statistics in economic analysis. And one well-known economist, Wanniski, says politics must be studied carefully as a market moving factor before all else.

Economist Reuven Brenner, in a recent book *Labyrinths of Prosperity*, noted the folly of basing public policy on statistics when a GNP growth number of 2.3% was "corrected" a month later to 3.9%, for a change of 70%. To use such a figure in any decision about policy, personal or public, is simple folly, he notes, at least until you know which is correct. Brenner's book is an old fashioned argument against government control of financial assets, personal and public, and the manipulation of statistics by public officials. Preoccupation with numbers is one way politicians turn prosperity into a labyrinth. That doesn't mean that bottom line numbers can be ignored. It means that obfuscation must be avoided. Some or much use of statistics in economic and other analysis, can be more misleading than enlightening.

Modern society is dominated by the need for investment capital, a skilled work force, a government that allows the use of capital to energize the work force, and access to education and natural resources. Communist countries, emerging from their dark histories, are demonstrating that while money may be the most basic need, you also need equally to make progress on all other fronts. Entrepreneurial skills are as vital as money, but so is a legal framework to protect investment capital and contracts. Russia demonstrates how difficult it is to progress simultaneously on all these fronts, especially for a huge country. The Czech Republic has made an almost complete recovery from its Communist tortures, but it is a tiny state and was under the dictatorship for a much shorter period of time than Russia. Poland, of all the other former communist entities, appears to be making long strides into industrial and commercial success. China, while retaining the outward trappings of a Communist dictatorship, has actually made a remarkable transition into capitalism, in the process controlling many of the traumas that beset the other emerging countries.

Where is the U.S. in this picture? We're the engine or locomotive of history, if you please. Without the U.S. economy, very little world progress is possible. It isn't just because we're the world's only military superpower, though that helps. It's because we're the world's only industrial and commercial superpower. Japan rivals us in some details, but not overall. One day China will surpass us, but not soon. Meanwhile U.S. investment capital resources and know-how control the world's markets, which in turn control the world's commerce and industry.

Many critics of U.S. policy, here and abroad, denounce U.S. success, pointing instead to our failures. But our failures are not necessarily financial or even educational, so much as they are political and cultural. Crime, for example, is cultural and political rather than financial. During the worst depression in history, beginning in 1929, crime rates remained a fraction of what they are today. Moreover, that was in a period when there were no social cushions or networks, no welfare, no social security or free medical care, no food stamps or aid for dependent children, no government grants for studying the habits of bees or persons with bees in their bonnets. There was no black underclass; we were all in it together. Our failures today are oddly disconnected from our successes. U.S. leadership in markets and investment with its impact on all the world's economies is only lightly touched by our gnawing crime and other problems. But it *is* touched and it ought to be a matter of government's highest concern that you can only do so much damage to the investment machine that makes the U.S. unique before it begins to creak and break down. Supporters of big government deny this without explaining why they should be believed. The reason? They have convinced plenty of voters who don't have access to investment capital—most individuals, unfortunately—that they are right. An earlier generation Kennedy, JFK, railed against big business, but he also chopped business taxes, thus stimulating economic growth. Later Kennedys advocated higher taxes.

Some critics of OEX trading and other, higher profile derivative instruments claim that such financial speculation corrupts the basic meaning and thrust of markets. Markets translate an economy's business into daily transactions by raising money for the economy as they reward individual and corporate investors. Indexes, in effect, or so it is claimed, sever this connection by turning into "mindless" (i.e. programmed by computer) trading or investing. Market performance should be related to company performance, otherwise incentive is lost along with any ethical connection between cause and effect.

This criticism was heard especially in the period of the 1987 market crash of 508 Dow points and the 190 point Dow decline of October 13, 1989. These were troubling, traumatic events that drove away millions of traditional investors. They were the lifeblood of the markets, therefore of the economy. What happens if they don't return?

Of course, they did return; the markets recovered and some would argue that the more-than-doubled market since those days is ample proof that the patient recovered fully. The safeguards ("collars") installed since then have cushioned the market against breaking down on several occasions when collapse seemed imminent. Moreover, all the studies of the big collapse in 1987 more or less exonerated options and other derivatives. Blame has yet to be fixed precisely. It's like trying to fix blame for the Great Depression. Schools of thought have grown up in both cases. I believe that options and program trading helped grease the skids, but the skids were there for economic reasons. Derivatives had nothing to do with that. OEX trading, at any rate, is a tiny segment of market speculation, meaning little beyond itself in the total world picture. Many billions of dollars circulate around world markets each day; OEX options are an insignificant part of that kitty.

The small investor returned mostly via the mutual fund. To the small investor, the "scattershot" approach of the mutual fund seems safer than the individual stock. When a market fall occurs, the fund manager is now the "fall guy." While speculating in the OEX is not investing, it is a variant of investing; it causes money to flow into the markets, hence into the economy, and the successful speculator is also usually a conservative investor.

Is computer trading "mindless?" Only if you believe a computer program to be mindless. Once a program is worked out, mastered and accepted, it does become mechanical. That's not mindless. It becomes simple repetition, like sorting fruit or washing cars, which are not occupations that inspire confidence in the economy or the individual. But it isn't mindless. New computer programs come constantly on stream, to take into account changes in markets and perceptions. Thus it represents a compression in time of things that once were spread out in time among different people.

Those who want to outlaw computerized trading in options and other derivatives need also to outlaw the computer. It might be a good idea but it won't fly. In fact, for decades communist societies restricted the use of computers to government bureaucrats. It was one of the reasons these societies failed.

Options are a challenge; so is democracy to a Haitian. Options are here to stay; so are critics of options. Every human activity has critics or enemies. So long as the critics of options don't start throwing bombs, they get their day in court. If the U.S. Congress begins to believe that this or that constituency (with a lot of votes) is dead set against OEX options, it will be time enough to grope for the panic button. Until then it is time to relax.

Trading in OEX options is not terribly complicated, but it does demand the right psychology, which is a mix of risk-taking not unlike any entrepreneurial impulse and closely related to any other market investment. So most of the decisions involved are highly rational. It is, however, both art and science, much like general economic analysis. For all its use of formulas and models, economics often is a highly subjective discipline, resembling philosophy, psychology and history in this respect. If it is partly an art, obviously it bears little resemblance to fine art or the decorative arts. Nothing in economics resembles a symphony or a painting (especially modern examples). For one thing, art is the work of a single individual at first, whereas economic events rarely depend on one person. But a U.S. president or other major world leader can often set events in motion that directly influence market movements, and the U.S. Federal Reserve chairman can cause market stampedes all over the world when he gets interest rates to rise or fall. Economics is mostly about investment theory and practice, about the world's money, not yours.

As I noted earlier, however, the world, in the form of governments—local, national and international—sees no difference between its money and yours. Big city and state governments add layers of taxes in bewildering amounts, despite the numbing effect these taxes have on the entrepreneurial system, the system that has vanquished the totalitarian dictatorship as the goal of all the world's desired form of government. Taxes go to pay for ever new entitlement programs for this or that special interest. In the long run such taxes debilitate the economy and lower its productive capacity.

Individuals anxious to preserve their own financial productivity must become as clever as the state in picking their pockets. Business and industry respond to government taxes and regulations by automating, relocating factories in less onerous parts of the world and cutting corners in every conceivable way (except over-paying their CEOs). The inevitable result is that jobs become scarcer and harder to find and hold, or they become less desirable and more pressurized.

One obvious way of enhancing financial independence and productivity is to master the art-science of financial speculation, as the big fund managers are able to do when they are successful. Mastering speculation, in addition to regular investment procedures with stocks, bonds, real estate and other traditional areas, can mean more money for more investment. The two approaches feed upon each other. If investment is the basis of the U.S. economy—and all others—then speculative investing has its key place within that sphere. Money flows from speculative activities into every other financial nook and cranny of the economy. Above all, if you succeed, it flows to you.

Only the U.S. and Japan have financial markets that attract large segments of the general population. Old European countries have their markets, but local public participation in them is slight compared to the U.S. and Japan. One reason for increasing U.S. interest is the subject of this book, the OEX, or to give it its full name, the S&P 100 options index.

Another reason, which brings us full circle in this introduction, is the changing nature of work. Unemployment the world over is rising, not falling, and work is becoming internationalized, like markets. Factories turn up everywhere though their owners may live in New York or London. The old ideas of work loyalty both by management and labor no longer operate. Increasingly it is every man and woman for themselves and the devil take the hindmost. Some people will say "it was never any different," but Japan for years had "lifetime employment" at least for one class of people, and that is eroding. In the U.S. one heard of generations of workers in the automobile industry. That too is vanishing.

New kinds of work are essential for survival in such a world, and market speculating (and investment) ought to be among them. It is educationally scandalous that young people learn nothing about economics or the stock market, but that is because the educational bureaucracy controls the curriculum and would rather teach what is currently fashionable. Nowadays that is "multi-culturalism," but who knows what it will be tomorrow. Meanwhile, there has been no appreciable gain in the U.S. standard of living for decades except for those people who can deal with the realities of modern economic life. Fortunately, there are ways of meeting the new challenges, posed by government with its taxes and restrictions, and industry with its frantic scramble for profitability. Among these ways is the OEX index.

C H A P T E R 1

Fundamentals

Fundamentals of the OEX

1. Risks and opportunities
2. Margin money
3. Time value
4. Definitions
5. Three usual markets
6. In-the-money and out-of-the-money stock
   options

Before the crash of 1987, the OEX had become one of the most popular trading baubles in Wall Street history. For very little margin cost—around $3,000 for the basic monthly strategy—you could receive a 100 percent return, and far more if you invested more. You could also lose far more if you used the wrong strategy in the 1987 crash and the 1989 quake.

However, the game has been changed because of heavy losses. Now, the entry cost for doing OEX strategies—combinations, straddles, and any strategy in which there is open-ended risk—has boomed up to about $50,000 in some places, and up to $100,000 in yet others. Other brokers charge far less—down to $25,000—but in any case the lunch is over. OEX traders in risky strategies must now have plenty of reserve cash if they wish to use combination strategies where there is open-ended risk. Therefore, this book offers a way around such hefty cash requirements. I have never believed that only the rich are entitled to be rich.

The crash that saw the end of the free lunch for options players, and the quake of October 13, 1989, when the Dow dropped 190 points in a perilous whiff of a replay of the crash, did teach several lessons for those who find experience a teacher.

If you owned put options and other bear market strategies in options, you would have made huge gains. If you had thereupon turned around and applied opposite strategies in the days, weeks and months following these market cataclysms, using calls and bull strategies, you would have made equally huge gains. Because market spectaculars—crises—must now be considered a normal aspect of computerized trading, the wise market player must know something about options. If you are an investor in mutual funds, thinking only of modest gains while protecting your nest egg, the fact is that the managers of these funds are using options and the S&P 500 to protect your money (and their jobs). Options and the S&P 500 are now woven into the fabric of the big funds, the real owners of the stock market in that they control about 60 percent of all its transactions, and on any day's trading as much as 90 percent.

About the only way the most cautious investor can avoid options and stock index futures is to buy government securities. As interest rates decline (if they do), that's like kissing your sister. An aging population that depends on dividends and interest in large part will need other resources.

That is not to say that widows and orphans must take up speculation in options. They must not, though any such person with a talent for it, and a few thousand dollars of speculative capital lying around in old shoe boxes, might check it out. It can be exhilarating and entertaining as well as profitable.

In this book you will find plenty of safe havens for idle dollars, with precise illustrations on how to use them, how to avoid losses, and what risks you can expect to encounter. All use of money entails some risk, from the buying of processed food that contains excessive salt for an unwary cardiac patient, to the money center bank that lends billions to a country that then declares bankruptcy. Options are far removed from these extremes, but they are not without their risks and rewards. You do have to eat something, and banks need to use some of their money speculatively. And some option strategies are almost without risk.

Shakespeare said "experience keeps a dear school but fools will learn in no other." He lived without the computer, a theoretical instrument without parallel. Its ability to absorb information, follow densely packed theoretical commands, and organize it all in an instant, is paradoxically an instrument of hands-on, transactional attitude. We now learn by observing the effects of computer programs on the information we ask them to absorb. So it is possible to generalize about the behavior of the market in ways that it was fanciful to do in the past. One such generalization tells us that after violent market episodes or crises—e.g., 1987 and 1989—it makes sense to believe that the market will settle into a much more placid behavior, probably with an upward bias. Thus the atmosphere invites spreading, an options technique we explore in detail that takes advantage of a market after its fall and when violence is wrung out of its system.

You might retort that common sense would also suggest such an outcome; all the selling is over, much of it in panic, and buyers are intimidated, fearful lest the aftershocks could contain more losses. Contempt for common sense is itself contemptible, but options have a few complexities that it would be unwise to ignore. The last two market crises offered case studies in the use and misuse of options. We do well to learn as much as possible from them, allowing for the unfortunate fact that market analysis is an occult art and a quasi-science.

The Risks, the Opportunities

In general, any strategy that hedges market direction— balancing loss against gain in sudden market moves—won't make you rich or poor. It won't make you much of anything. But there are exceptions to every generalization. If you had an equal number of puts and calls on October 19, 1987, when the Dow dropped 508 points, you would have made an enormous amount of money on your puts, and had only minor losses on your calls. Moreover, had you turned around the next morning and bought more calls, the profits on the new ones would have also been enormous, far outweighing the losses the day before. You may say "that's hindsight." Yes it is, but it has happened often enough to become hardened into a rule; hedging market direction with OEX puts and calls is an essential strategy in computer driven markets. It is emphatically indicated in markets of high volatility such as we have seen in any period where economic and political uncertainty prevail.

Hedging can be employed in various ways. Selling covered options on stocks you own is a form of hedging. The money you receive when you sell options on your stock hedges against a portion of the drop in the price of the stock. There are risks; if you sell calls and the stock goes up past the strike price of the call, you will lose the appreciation beyond the strike price. Appreciation loss is as real as any other.

Buying stocks and selling calls on them also risks the cost of the transaction. You can undertake this strategy often enough to cost a hefty part of the profits. Moreover, the amount of profit isn't more than a few percentage points of the price of the stock, easily chewed up by transaction costs. Thus, selling covered options on stock you own has been a good strategy in the past, when some stocks had fat premiums in their options that made annual gains of 50 percent a possibility. Today it is difficult to find such stocks. Option premiums are no longer so rich; indeed, compared with their lurid past, they are almost an underclass. So, selling covered calls on your favorite stocks, while not terribly risky, has lost some of its former luster, unless you own large amounts of a single stock with good option premiums and are willing to take the risk of having the stock appreciate and being called away.

Suppose you own 1,000 shares of Apple Computer, a stock that DOES have a good option premium and thus is a candidate for the strategy of covered option "writes" (sales). As of this writing Apple Computer is selling at 34 1/2. You could sell 1,000 calls at a strike price of 35, three and a half months until expiration, and receive $3,000 for your trouble (the option is at 3). You could hope to do that three times a year, if the stock doesn't go above 35. The market rarely obliges the best laid plans of mice and men. While it is going down at this point, it will certainly go up soon after this chapter is written. It will take your Apple stock from you, at which point you probably could find another candidate and go through the same exercise—and profit. You might then, with 1,000 shares of a similarly priced stock and option, make close to $9,000 on your investment of $35,000, or about 26 percent. You could use the same tactic with half that much stock. Below 500 shares you face commission costs of consequence to your trade.

You need a conscientious, wide-awake broker for such trading. These qualifications are contradictions in terms; if they are wide awake they have no conscience save their pocketbook, and if they are good they graduate to easier jobs (options are tough).

The risks in this bland, apparently riskless strategy are that the market could collapse and your stock could lose a large percentage of its worth. If you sold, just to get out of it, you would lose at least part of the money you gained when you sold the calls. These are risks one can live with; the stock market goes up as well as down.

To pursue this strategy you want a stock that has a good option premium and a low *beta* (it doesn't move much, regardless of what every other stock is doing). On any given day there are few such candidates. Though this strategy has nothing to do with the OEX (our main subject), it is one that has opportunities from time to time, given the right broker or your own persistence.

There are other instances where options can be used similarly.

If you follow the market closely, studying up on individual stocks, you may learn that XYZ Company is about to buy back a large block of stock. You don't need to own XYZ stock to rush out and buy in-the-money or at-the-money calls, risking a few hundred or a few thousand dollars on near-term plays. Or you may read about another company whose fortunes are declining for reasons over which they have no control. Then you buy puts on their stock, again at-the-money or in-the-money.

Similar possibilities pertain to the entire market, only here the best instrument to use is the OEX.

I have opposed buying individual or five-lot (etc.) OEX options on the often repeated statistic that buyers of options lose money about 80 percent of the time. Yet how many of these buyers actually know what they are doing? No statistics are available on this not irrelevant matter. So if you are willing to do some digging before you jump into that 80 percent hole, you might be able to land on your feet in triumph.

We are talking here about market timing. Can anybody actually time the market well enough to be making money on it? Everybody who claims to be able to do it makes whopping errors but goes right on claiming success. Perhaps success in this field should be measured as it is among big league batters—if you are right (i.e., get a hit) once in every three attempts you are considered a genius. The market timer needs to get one of three possible directions right. There are several sections in this book on market timing for those who would like to enter the field. Your attention should also be directed to the Financial News Network.

Remember that when you buy an option, your entire risk is the price you pay plus commission. It's only when you sell an option, without hedging it, that you risk much more.

Selling combinations trapped many people during the 1987 crash. What happens is you lose far more on the collapsing side than you gain on the other side. We outline the risks, later.

Selling options (called "writing" options) always entails more risk, hence more margin or "up front" money, as there are more opportunities for profit. The amount of risk can be judged by the losses in the various market breaks in 1987, 1989 and 1990. Those who sold the wrong options—puts, individually or in an index such as the OEX or MMI—lost huge sums. Those who sold calls did well, but not extraordinarily so. When the market collapses, calls decline, but if you sold them you wouldn't make more than the original amount specified for the strike price. But BUYERS of puts make out like bandits in huge collapses, while buyers of calls lose whatever they put into calls—no more.

It follows that in volatile markets you need to buy both puts and calls and the key is the amount of volatility. The key to that is our old bugaboo, market timing. It's a subject that needs constant reinventing because today's super special indicator is tomorrow's big bust. You have only to check out the timing career of Joe Granville. Granville's crystal ball (and his "on-balance volume" indicators) went "south" while the market went "north" in 1982. Granville was unable to reverse direction until the bull market had almost run its course. Predicting market direction is a dangerous profession.

Not everyone was wrong at crucial moments. A well-known Wall Street broker, Elaine Garzarelli, had the crash figured out perfectly and on time to do something about it. So did Lynn Elgert, a columnist for the *Hume MoneyLetter.* There were others. But perhaps it is more important to be able to figure out when the market is about to go UP. After all, a panic reaction to the crash that made you sell all your stocks at a big loss, was precisely the wrong course to take. Good stocks, almost without exception, recovered all their losses eventually, and went on to new highs. To be sure, if you could have sold BEFORE the crash, and bought back at the bottom, around 1750, and held on for the next top above 2800, you would have been (1) a genius, (2) gifted with fool's luck, and (3) rich. It is well to be all three.

The options player going through crashes with the wrong instrument is like the super tanker pilot who is floundering but can't do much about the thing causing the trouble. According to environmentalists and others, super tankers are always the wrong instruments; just so, many financial observers make the same charge against options for similar reasons (polluting their environment).

In addition to the risks cited above with OEX and other options, there is also the risk peculiar to trading in combinations—spreads, straddles, etc. That is the complexity risk, which covers not only the juggling aspect in which you must understand the meaning of market moves on several differing positions you own, but also the difficulty of getting the right transactions executed at the time you specify.

If you have a perfect broker you won't have problems. If, however, you happen to live in the real world, there will be problems. Your broker will be out to lunch, on vacation, be pressed with other duties, or not terribly interested in your account. There is always an increased risk of exposure to market whiplash when one side of the combination is closed out and the other side remains in force and you haven't replaced the closed side properly. A malevolent options god waits for such situations, pouncing on an optioneer out to make a killing in such a situation rather than merely exiting gracefully. This evil spirit juggles the market in hostile moves on your position—almost invariably.

In straddles where you write both a put and a call, you are exposed to unlimited risk if the market goes against both sides of the straddle. Straddles (sometimes called strangles) are always risky, especially if they are close to being in- or at-the-money. If you are doing this with options on a stock, the risk level is not quite as high. Any time the stock violates the strike price the stock will be exercised (sold). You rescue such positions with fancy footwork, but it isn't easy.

In market crashes—the crises—there has been a kind of financial gridlock. They were calling it "meltdown" where transactions never took place, where phones were jammed or unanswered, brokers couldn't handle orders, market makers were terror-stricken and more or less catatonic, as if the Exchange had been overrun by the Viet Cong in a revival. Such events, commonplace in 1987, are not supposed to happen again. The tooth fairy will not allow it.

Such risks as these inhere in every financial transaction, even in government bonds where interest rate changes create changes in the value of the bonds. But every risk also contains an opportunity. And that is where options come in; within their mercurial bounds there lie both risk and opportunity.

Use of Margin Money

Trading the OEX requires a margin account. If you are only buying options there are no margin costs, and in the several hedging strategies we advocate, the margin required is minimal, about $5,000 for five contracts. Selling naked options —strangles—is high risk and high margin—up to $100,000 and as low as $20,000. Margin money can be in stock and bond certificates of yours kept by the broker.

OEX Time Value

Time value and intrinsic or "real" value are keys to successful OEX trading. The more time that remains before the combination's expiration date, the more value it has. But the remaining time is also your enemy. Disasters are enacted in time. The disaster potential—the crisis—is what makes it vital to take and be satisfied with any halfway respectable profit, no matter what time has elapsed or remains. If any rule of thumb can be inferred from options trading it is: take profits gladly and quickly for losses are sure to follow. Options trading, like commodities, always involves some loss, especially in those strategies where loss is built in. Anyone who "can't bear to lose" has no business trading options. Good options traders minimize losses.

Definitions

Combinations or spreads occur when you buy or sell both sides of the OEX—puts and calls. You can sell one side and buy the other, sell both sides, or buy both sides. You can also have different time values within the same trade. The sale of both sides, since the 1987 crash, is frowned upon in prudent circles. It is only to be undertaken by options high-rollers, or highly informed rollers— a different case. Within all these groupings there are many variations. You can use the same or different months; you can sell or buy more heavily on one side than on the other; you can use widely different strike prices.

The terms straddle and spreads may be used instead of combination. Some brokers use them interchangeably. However, the Chicago Board of Options defines a combination as a straddle with a differing number of puts and calls. If you sell ten calls and five puts, or vice versa, you have a combination, whereas in a straddle you sell the same number.

Another term, strangle, is also used. It sometimes simply denotes a straddle of a particular kind—the sale of both sides of a combination, which is the most dangerous of all types, and the most expensive also (highest margin costs). Strangles also may refer to your fate if you misuse them.

The risks in selling both sides were demonstrated too abundantly in the crash. It's a strategy to use with caution.

The Three Usual Markets

The use of option strategies with a single stock has been spurned by many investors who said they didn't understand them, or that losses could be large and unpredictable. Because the OEX is an index instrument based on a composite of 100 blue chip stocks, it is not subject to the vagaries of a single stock option. But to take advantage of the OEX, you must know how to utilize it in each of the three usual markets—up, down, sideways.

Different markets require different strategies. You may say that it is impossible to predict the future and therefore future markets, so a book describing the way the OEX worked in the past isn't necessarily going to be helpful in the future. It is true that markets don't repeat exactly. The bull market that started in August 1982, differed from all previous bull markets in both its movement and volume.

But some things never change. Markets move in only two directions—up and down—or they don't move at all, but go sideways. Indeed, sideways is the way they move most of the time.

If you chart stock markets over the past five or ten years, the most noticeable kind of market is a "trading range" market. That's one in which the Dow Jones Industrial Average (the Dow)—the most quoted of all market indicators—moves within a fairly narrow trading range. In recent years the range was about 100 points. The Dow would move approximately 100 points up and 100 points down over a period of months. The Dow would then move above or below the range briefly, perhaps establishing a new trading range slightly above or below the old one. Increments of change in the markets were much less volatile than at present when we have greater volume, largely due to the computer and program trading.

Percentage of change, however, does not differ from years gone by. When a rise or drop of 50 points or more takes place, causing consternation and big headlines, the percentage of change is not all that different. A 10 or 15 point movement in a market trading in the Dow range of 800 is about the same percentage as a 20 or 30 point movement in the 1600 range. So the French saying "the more things change, the more they remain the same" is a measure of the usefulness of a strategy based on the past. If percentage change in trading isn't all that different, it follows that you can erect strategies to guide your money through various market behaviors.

After the October 19, 1987, crash in the market, when over 500 Dow points were lost in the single worst day in market history, there were many cries to reform the market, and to outlaw program trading, a process in which arbitragers take advantage of discrepancies between stock index futures and the cash price of the stocks represented by the futures to lock in instant profits. Program trading was indeed suspended. There were even calls to curtail OEX and other stock index trading, though most complaints were against the S&P 500 stock index futures, the chief instrument of arbitrage, along with stocks and options on futures.

The complaint should be made against the computer, which made such trading possible. But the U.S. Congress really can't outlaw computers.

When so enormous an event as the market crash of October 1987 occurs, the need for explanation and the pinpointing of villains becomes a major industry. Without attempting to deny that program trading has fed market volatility, and with it a domination of the market by the big institutional players who use arbitrage and portfolio insurance (another use of futures and options), the fact remains that there was little program trading on October 19, 1987. There wasn't any on the two days that followed in which the market rocketed upwards to new records in Dow advances. New villains will have to be discovered, but it all comes back to the computer and its works. Meanwhile, the OEX *should* be used in any kind of market, both for big players and small. That is its democratic virtue. The techniques and tactics I describe in this book will help investors protect themselves. Using these they can take advantage of seemingly disastrous circumstances. These strategies will work in good and bad times.

That is the crux of this book—coping with market changes using the OEX. There are many OEX strategies that one might use, but I want to keep to a manageable few which are productive and not high risk. I will also heed the admonition of the medieval philosopher Occam, who warned future generations to "avoid multiplying entities needlessly," which in modern phrasing is KISS or "keep it simple, stupid."

This book will present a step-by-step explanation, using

many real world examples, of the several OEX trading strategies to use in different markets. For those who want to take one
additional step, we also explain the S&P 500 stock index
futures contract. The OEX strategies have been winners about
75 percent of the time; the S&P 500 about 60 percent. The goal
is to make winning totals equal winning percentages. There is
no profit in small winnings 75 percent of the time and big
losses 25 percent of the time.

OEX strategies include the selling of combinations or
straddles, the buying of combinations, and the use of a combination buy-sell strategy, all in various kinds of markets. We
combine all these strategies in certain kinds of situations, as
well as other strategies such as vertical spreads.

As to the S&P 500 futures contract, we offer our strategy
for using it in those rare situations—ten times a year or so—
when it offers great opportunities.

Option Fundamentals

The S&P 100, symbol OEX, is an option index based on 100
Standard & Poor stocks. It made its debut in 1983, trading on
the Chicago Board Options Exchange (CBOE). It has dominated all option play since then, draining interest away from
individual stock options, as well as other competing financial
instruments such as stock index futures and other option indexes. To lay the groundwork for trading the OEX, we will
examine individual stock options. If you are already familiar
with options trading you may want to skip to chapter 2.

The purchase of an option on a single stock gives you the
right but not necessarily the obligation to buy that stock. There
are two kinds of options, puts and calls. One call entitles its
owner to buy 100 shares of the indicated stock at a specified
price and within a specified period of time, all of which you may
look up in the *Wall Street Journal.* Thus: a Mobil Nov 35, 15/16
call, entitles its owner to buy 100 shares of Mobil at any time

N.Y. Stock Exchange

NYSE INDEX OPTIONS

Strike	Calls—Last			Puts—Last		
Price	Sep	Oct	Nov	Sep	Oct	Nov
160	....	....	....	....	3/8	....
165	11 1/4	....	....	1/8	1	....
170	6 1/4	....	....	1/2	2 3/16	3 5/8
175	2 5/8	5 5/8	7 3/8	1 13/16	4	5 3/4
177 1/2	1 1/4	....	....	0 1/4	....	....
180	11/16	3 1/16	5 1/2	5 1/2	6 5/8	....
182 1/2	1/4	2 1/4	....	7 3/16	....	....
185	1/8	1 5/8	3 3/8	9 3/4	11	11 1/2
187 1/2	1/16	1 1/8	....	11 5/8	....	....
190	....	11/16	2 1/8	....	....	....
192 1/2	1/16	1/2	....	....	....	....
195	....	3/8	1 3/8	....	....	....
197 1/2	....	5/16				
200	....	3/16				

Total call volume 4,500. Tot
Total put volume 4,366. Tot
The index: High 176.48; L

NYSY

Strike	Calls—Last	
Price	Sep	Oct
370	....	....
380	....	11 1/4
390	1 1/4	....
395	5/8	....

Total call volume 28. Total
Total put volume 13. Total
The index: High 381.09; L

Chicago Board

S&P 100 INDEX

Strike	Calls—Last			Puts—Last		
Price	Sep	Oct	Nov	Sep	Oct	Nov
260	50	....	....	....	....	....
275	....	....	....	1/16	....	....
280	31 1/2	....	....	1/16	....	....
285	....	28	29 1/4	1/8	7/8	2
290	22 3/4	23 1/2	26	3/16	1 1/2	2 7/8
295	17 1/2	19	23	3/8	2 9/16	4
300	11 3/4	15 1/2	19 1/4	13/16	3 5/8	5 7/8
305	7 5/8	12 1/4	16	1 7/8	5 1/8	7 5/8
310	4 3/8	9 1/8	13 1/2	3 5/8	7 1/4	9 3/4
315	2 1/8	7	10 1/4	6 3/8	10	12 3/4
320	1	4 7/8	8 1/2	10 1/2	12 7/8	14 1/2
325	1/2	3 3/8	6 1/2	15 1/2	16 1/2	18
330	1/4	2 1/4	5 1/8	20	20 1/2	23 1/8
335	1/8	1 1/2	3 5/8	25	24 1/2	26 1/2
340	1/16	1	3	28 1/2	29	30
345	1/16	5/8	2 1/2	34	33 3/8	....
350	1/16	3/8	1 9/16	....	....	....

Total call volume 231,447 Total call open int. 810,291
Total put volume 187,058 Total put open int. 745,390
The index: High 311.89; Low 308.75; Close 310.06, −0.14.

S&P 500 INDEX

Strike	Calls—Last			Puts—Last		
Price	Sep	Oct	Dec	Sep	Oct	Dec
295	....	....	....	3/16	2	5 1/8
300	13 1/2	....	....	7/16	....	6 3/4
305	10 3/8	15	....	1 1/16	4 1/2	....
310	6 1/4	....	16 1/2	2 1/2	6 3/8	9 7/8
315	3 5/8	8 3/8	14	4 3/8	8 1/8	13 1/4
320	1 3/4	6 1/2	12	7 5/8	10 3/4	14 1/2
325	13/16	4 3/4	10	12 1/2	14 1/2	17 1/4
330	3/8	3	....	15 7/8	....	....
335	3/16	2 1/4	6 3/4	21	....	....
340	1/16	1 1/2	5 3/4	26 3/8	....	....
345	1/16	1 1/8	4 1/2	31 1/4	....	....
350	....	3/4	4	....	....	....
355	....	3/8	3 1/8	....	....	....

Total call volume 8,330 Total call open int. 219,507
Total put volume 6,507 Total put open int. 233,288
The index: High 315.41; Low 312.29; Close 313.92, +0.36.

The S&P 100 Index, S&P 500 Index, and the NYSE Index Options boxes from Sept. 9, 1987.

OPTION PRICE		DECIMAL VALUE		DOLLAR VALUE	OPTION PRICE		DECIMAL VALUE		DOLLAR VALUE
1/16	=	.0625	=	$ 6.25	9/16	=	.5625	=	$ 56.25
1/8	=	.1250	=	$12.50	5/8	=	.6250	=	$ 62.50
3/16	=	.1875	=	$18.75	11/16	=	.6875	=	$ 68.75
1/4	=	.2500	=	$25.00	3/4	=	.7500	=	$ 75.00
5/16	=	.3125	=	$31.25	13/16	=	.8125	=	$ 81.25
3/8	=	.3750	=	$37.50	7/8	=	.8750	=	$ 87.50
7/16	=	.4375	=	$43.75	15/16	=	.9375	=	$ 93.75
1/2	=	.5000	=	$50.00	1	=	1.0000	=	$100.00

Converting fractions from the options charts into dollar values can be puzzling. Here's a fraction-decimal-dollar chart to help out.

before the third Friday in November at the strike price of $35 plus commissions and the cost of the option. In this case it would be 15/16 of 1—meaning $100—or approximately $93.75.

A put entitles its owner to sell 100 shares of the indicated stock, also at a specified price within a specified period of time. Thus: a Mobil 25 Nov, 7/8 put, entitles its owner to sell, or "put to" its buyer, 100 shares of Mobil stock at the strike price of $25 plus commissions and the cost of the option, which is $87.50 (7/8 of 1 or $100).

The point of buying a call instead of the underlying stock is because the call typically costs hundreds of dollars, whereas the stock itself costs thousands. If you believe that Mobil* stock will go up in price sharply, the price of the call will rise correspondingly, thus enabling the owner of the call to sell it at a profit. When this happens the owner of the call will not exercise his right to buy the stock. When he closes out the call he has made his profit. There is no obligation and it would be foolish to do so since the stock is now increased in price. Of course the person who originally sold the call to him now has the obligation to buy Mobil at the new, increased price, in effect

* (*Note:* Mobil is picked for these illustrations because it is a conservative stock, offering average opportunities in options rather than a more active, and volatile stock. The actual price of Mobil stock will change, but the ideas will remain the same.)

taking a loss on the call he sold. He will usually buy back the call at a loss, instead of buying the stock and then selling it at a loss (i.e., at a higher price than he could have bought it earlier). He had sold the call in the belief and hope that Mobil would decline in price and he would get to keep the premium he received in the sale of it. But in our example, the seller of the call lost and the buyer won, which isn't the usual case at all. There are ways to avoid some or all of the loss, as we will see later.

When a put is bought, the purchaser believes that Mobil will decline sharply in price, inflating the price of the put, which may then be sold at a profit before expiration. Remember that an option is a wasting asset that expires in a fixed period of time. One additional reason for buying a put, not present in the call purchase: the owner of the put already owns Mobil stock and buys the put as insurance against its decline. Each put covers 100 shares of stock. The stock owner, believing Mobil is going down but not wanting to sell the stock (doesn't want to give up the hefty dividend, thinks the stock has long-term possibilities) buys the put as insurance against a decline. If the stock is owned at $25 or more, the put will appreciate in value as the stock declines, dollar for dollar, if Mobil goes below 25.

The above discussion is partly theoretical, but also partly real. In the time period specified (around November 1986), Mobil never dropped to 25 or lower. So the buyer of the put would have lost the entire amount of each put ($87.50), plus commissions.

In-the-Money Stock Options

The buyer of the call, by contrast, would have made money. How much depends on when the call was cashed in. The specified price in the put and call definitions is called the strike price, and the specified time is usually a three month period with a closing expiration date, always the third Friday of the specified month.

Mobil actually touched 39 for a day or two in the November 1986 period, meaning that the 35 call strike price was briefly 4 points, or $400 in-the-money. (*In-the-money* refers to the difference between the higher price of the stock at 39 and the lower strike price of the 35 call, which provides a profit of 4 points.) The owner of the call could have made that $400 per call plus whatever time value (distance from expiration date) the call had at the time she took profit. Time value is determined by the market; as option expiration date nears, time value collapses and disappears at expiration date. But from five to six weeks or more prior to expiration date, time value can be either fractional, or whole points (multiplying the number of points by $100 gives the dollar value of the option), depending on how much buying and selling there is in the option. Mobil options generally have low time values because of the low volatility of Mobil stock. It doesn't move much, so neither do the options, which thrive on volatility.

In addition to time value, options have real or intrinsic value—when they are in-the-money. Put another way, with Mobil at $38 per share, a Nov call with a strike price of 35 would be $3 (times 100) or 3 points in-the-money. As noted, in-the-money is the difference between the higher present price of the stock and the lower strike price of the call. That intrinsic value of $3 or 3 points doesn't change with time, as does the time value of the option; rather it changes with the price of the stock. An in-the-money call goes up in value when the stock moves up, no matter how little time remains before expiration, or down in value when the stock price declines. (Also see glossary for at-the-money, which is the dividing line between in- and out-of-the-money options.)

Out-of-the-Money Stock Options

An out-of-the-money call will *always* decrease in value as expiration day approaches, unless at the end the stock price is nearing an in-the-money range. Being out-of-the-money is the same as saying the option lacks intrinsic or real in-the-money value. It has only time value. The Mobil Nov 35 call would be out-of-the-money if Mobil stock dropped from $38 per share to $34, or lower, and thus be below the strike price of 35. The 25 Nov put would be out-of-the-money if Mobil stock was higher than $25 per share. The stock price must be higher than the put strike price for the put to be out-of-the-money. The stock price must be lower than the put price for the put to be in-the-money. Here, with Mobil stock at $24, the 25 Nov put would be in-the-money by one point or $100 per put.

In the cases we've discussed we are dealing with individual (Mobil) stock options bought for speculative purposes in the case of the call, and for speculation and insurance in the case of the put. Each case, though, is based on some beliefs and hopes about Mobil and its stock. In summary, let us evaluate the potential gains and losses for these transactions in the actual time frame in which they could have occurred.

The buyer of the Mobil 25 Nov put would have lost the entire amount of the put ($87.50) times the number of puts he bought plus commissions, assuming that he held it until expiration date. That's because Mobil never fell to 25 or lower. But a smart options trader would not have held the put to the bitter end but would have taken a smaller loss well before expiration, when it was apparent that the put wasn't going anywhere.

The buyer of the Mobil Nov 35 call would have made money, how much would have depended on when the call was cashed in. Mobil actually touched 39 for a day or two during the period. So the 35 call was briefly 4 points in-the-money. The owner of the call, acting nimbly, could have made $400 on each call, minus commissions and the original cost of each call.

Not bad, not good, either, since the call owner had to be exactly right about the market, about Mobil, and about the time period. It's perfectly possible to be right about one of these three aspects of this equation. You could be right about the time period, and maybe even about the direction of Mobil and its price, but realistically your chances of getting all three precisely right are not great. They are, in fact, about 20 to 25 percent. The percentage of winning stock call buyers has been tracked by many people and institutions, and their findings keep coming out in that range. It follows that call *sellers* will profit 75 to 80 percent of the time. But hold on—you have to make enough to offset the 20 to 25 percent losses, and that's where the OEX comes in. The OEX does not depend on a single stock such as Mobil, but on 100 stocks more or less like Mobil.

One might think that it's easier to be right about one stock like Mobil than about 100 stocks similar to it, but 100 blue chip stocks offer a more diversified base than just one stock. With that part of the equation providing a better profile of stocks, you need only be concerned about the direction of the market and its trading range. OEX strategies make that more possible than trading with a single stock option.

An index option, in contrast with an individual stock option like the Mobil options, deals entirely in cash. Settlement is in cash, unlike the stock option where settlement may find the stock "put to" the seller or "called away" from the option speculator who owns a stock. Otherwise, the OEX (and other indexes such as the Amex Major Market Index) behave more or less like the Mobil option, allowing the differences noted and those to emerge later. An OEX in-the-money option is defined as before with the stock option; so too is an OEX put. But now let us turn to the OEX itself to learn about the important differences, and as the French say in another context, "long may they live."

Mobil, more recently, has traded in the low 80s, but all the relationships described above remain the same.

Exactly similar considerations apply to what follows—the OEX and its inner workings.

CHAPTER 2

Flexibility
and Safety

The OEX is preferred by traders over single stock options because:

1. Profits as large as 100 percent are possible on a small investment, which is less often possible with stock options.
2. There are more frequent opportunities to take profits (every month and under certain circumstances almost weekly).
3. Profits can be made when the market moves sideways, as well as up and down.
4. There is less risk because losses can be calculated in advance and can be limited using tactics described herein.
5. Market diversification obtained with the OEX also decreases risk. With single stock options you are at the mercy of many fundamental forces, such as a bad quarter, overseas political problems, domestic news of one sort or another, and news specific to the company. The OEX reflects the market as a whole.

The OEX

You find the OEX listing under the heading INDEX OPTIONS in the *Wall Street Journal*. On a typical day OEX lists strike prices covering 100 points, e.g., from 365 to 465 in the usual increments of 5. It takes about 7 Dow points to move the OEX 1 point.

The Chicago Board Options Exchange computes the OEX by taking the current market price of each stock in the index and multiplying it by its number of outstanding shares. The results are added to obtain the aggregate market value of all stocks in the OEX. The current value of the OEX is computed by dividing the aggregate market value by the base value and multiplying by 100. The OEX base value initially was based on the aggregate market value of the 100 stocks on January 2, 1976. Base values are now adjusted to reflect mergers, acquisitions, splits, and other changes. Each point on the OEX is equal to $100.

The OEX box lists three trading months for calls and puts, e.g., Nov Dec Jan (that's the way these months are abbreviated). Calls and puts are listed separately.

The highest prices on November 3, 1986, were the Nov and Dec 205 calls at 25 3/4, or $2,575 (the strike price, 25 3/4 times 100). Would anyone be buying these calls? Probably not, but plenty of people would be holding them or selling them based on lucky purchases when the market was lower. The Dow had been around 1740 in September, which means you could have bought such an OEX call 22 points lower (subtract Dow 1740, the low, from the closing Dow 1894, which is 154 Dow points, divided by 7). So, back in September, you might have "taken a flyer" and bought OEX calls that were 3 3/4, or $375 each. On November 4, 1986, they were worth $2,575 per call plus a time value of slightly over 1, giving a total of about $2,700 minus commissions.

How often can one expect to buy a call option at $375 and turn it into $2,700 in three months? Almost never, with the exception of a moving bull market that you catch precisely as it is moving. Remember that markets most often go sideways, and it is rare that you can hitch a ride on a shooting star. But it is much easier to do than trying to catch a move in a Mobil call. Remember also that an option is a wasting asset; time is literally of the essence, and with the OEX, we deal in one-to-three month time periods. Mobil calls move only when the stock moves, which isn't very often. OEX calls move far more often thanks to the sensitivity of the 100 blue chip OEX stocks, which in effect stand for the whole New York Stock Exchange (NYSE). They reflect the movements of the 1,500 or so stocks on the NYSE more or less exactly as the Dow does. There are exceptions in the way it moves, though. Sometimes, when the market moves 7 to 15 points, and you expect the OEX to move 1 or 2 points automatically, because of the ratio of 7 Dow points to 1 OEX, you may be puzzled to see that the correlation breaks down. The OEX may move less or more (but rarely very much) because it is a value-weighted index, with greater weight going to big capitalization stocks—those companies with more shares outstanding. So, on a day when the Dow moves 15 points and IBM doesn't move at all or even declines a bit, the chances are great that the OEX won't make the precise move you expect. That would be especially true if on such a day IBM were to be joined by several other big cap stocks.

The main action in the OEX is not in the extreme strike prices—the 1/16 or 25 3/4 numbers—but in strike prices much closer to the closing price, in this case 231.95. So note the prices of those puts and calls 5, 10 or 15 points above or below the 231.95 closing rather than those farther away. Here you see that a Nov 235 call costs 1 7/16, the Nov 240 call costs 7/16, the 230 Nov put costs 3 1/4, and the 225 Nov put costs 1 9/16.

Note also the difference time makes, time being the number of weeks from expiration. The OEX has monthly expiration dates, compared to quarterly expiration of stock options (though some stock options expire in monthly intervals also). It is this invariable monthly expiration feature that interests us constantly, because it offers constant opportunities. It recalls Shaw's description of marriage as offering the maximum of temptation with the maximum of opportunity.

Speculation is its Name

Perhaps a brief pause is in order to state precisely what we are doing when we trade the OEX, other option indexes, or stock options. We are speculating, though there are one or two non-speculative aspects to options that we will discuss later, such as hedging stocks or portfolios and the writing of covered options, a form of hedging.

There are many things to be said about option speculation in an age characterized by insider trading scandals, takeover trauma, and the incessant drumbeat of propaganda against capitalist markets from the political left (though most communist countries are attempting to smuggle some variant of these markets into their gasping economies). Speculators are not writing the *Ninth Symphony, Madame Butterfly* or *War and Peace.* What they are doing is adding liquidity to markets and seeking profits for investments. The creation of profit is what separates starving societies from those that thrive. Because the world is full of starving societies, or those close to starvation, every successful society—no matter its politics—needs to be nurtured with exquisite care. Every individual who contributes to profitability in such a society must be counted in the ranks of benefactors, however rich or poor such a person might be. This is not sentimentality; it is fact. No matter how many soup kitchens you underwrite, you are not adding to societal profitability. Instead, you may be decreasing it, since the encouragement of indigence merely adds to unprofitability. (Not all hungry people are indigent.)

What, you may say, has happened to Christian charity or compassion? The urge to help people is the noblest of mankind's legacies, alas it is too little practiced or understood. Nuns do it routinely; many other groups and individuals have kept the ideal alive in every age and society, including those of the modern world. But how are people best helped? Stop-gap measures are always essential and often available in most (but not all) societies, unless war or revolution is occurring. Long-term compassion is more helpful; it creates hope along with help, whereas soup kitchens create no hope. They kill it. Nurturing hope is the highest form of compassion, and only the creation of profit can begin the long climb toward a hopeful society.

To some people speculation is not far removed from sin. Yet speculation is at the heart of all entrepreneurship. Is it wicked? Foolish? It's risky, but less so than leaving your money in stocks that fall from the heights, or in bank accounts that don't keep up with inflation. Jimmy Carter, a U.S. president closely identified with morality in politics, pronounced speculation wicked. Theologians of Marxism and other conspicuous beliefs have joined in the condemnation from time to time. But evil, like beauty, is much in the eye of the beholder. Experts in evil are, however, the last to be trusted, since expertise in this field is often acquired in ways that arouse deep suspicion.

Speculation in financial and other futures contracts is a method of arriving at prices that interested individuals consider fair. They may be outrageously unfair when the contract's expiration date arrives, but when future prices are controlled by politicians the results are almost inevitably unfair, i.e., unacceptable to most interested parties. When the price of a thing is considered unacceptable, unfair, or outrageous, it may lead to various kinds of behavior, including the sort that leading moralists might condemn. This will not happen, or rarely so, when prices are set by free market mechanisms.

Speculation is a daily fixing of prices by market forces —speculators. It may be both fair and unfair, because many people are involved, but that is a commercial rather than a moral question. There are points of interaction between these kinds of questions, but each connection must be judged on its own. If speculation leads to bankruptcy and the starvation of children it is wicked, but if it leads to prosperity and reduces child starvation it is good. Once past these generalizations it is not easy to assess the morality of speculation. But it is obvious that considerations of morality have little to tell us about succeeding in financial futures speculation.

The Bottom Line

The considerations that should immediately attract your attention to OEX speculation are: 1. you may earn a profit up to 100 percent of your initial investment within a few weeks; 2. you can profit no matter what the market does; 3. you can profit frequently using the strategies in this book—once or twice a week when the market cooperates, which is not infrequent; 4. the initial investment for some OEX speculation isn't much more than $5,000, though the separate S&P 500 stock index futures speculation requires $50,000.

Let's resume our inspection of the OEX November 4, 1986, box. Why concentrate so long on something that will never recur exactly as it stood on that date? Because one cannot be certain that the Dow won't spend a lot of time in the general area of the November 4, 1986, box, and each time the market approaches that area the numbers won't be far away from the ones we are looking at. It isn't necessary that they be identical for them to be meaningful, in any case, and it really doesn't matter where the Dow rests. But remember that the

Dow spent years hitting 1000 and backing away from it. Had there been an OEX in those years it would have had many recurring numbers.

The OEX and Other Option Indexes

The OEX is an option index (a compilation of options) whereas individual stock options are appendages of their underlying stocks. The OEX index is based on 100 stocks; the single stock option on one. One should rarely use the strategies recommended in this book on single stock options, though it is perfectly possible to do so in some cases. With the wrong stock it would also be perfectly risky. The OEX, however, is risky about one-fourth of the time—a calculable risk. Individual stock options depend on news that can affect a single stock—like an overseas disaster, or a bad quarter, or a political change that affects a single company. The OEX, in contrast, is largely protected from such events. It tracks the market as a whole.

Option indexes have appeared from various sources. The American Exchange Major Market Index (XMI) was formed out of stocks that follow the Dow closely. It contains some of the Dow components. It's an interesting adjunct to the OEX.

The S&P 500 Index relates commodities to stocks, specifically the financial commodity called the S&P 500 stock index futures to a stock index based on a commodity. It's a financial futures commodity. Where the OEX moves in accordance with the rise and fall of the 100 blue chip stocks that support it, the S&P 500 Index moves rapidly, even treacherously, to rival the speed of pork bellies futures movements, hitherto the fastest. Traders refer to the S&P 500 futures as "pork bellies in pin stripes." Anyone who has traded the S&P 500 stock index futures knows the sweatiness of it; the furious movement up and down in an otherwise "normal" trading day. So why do we advocate it? It's a highly selective advocacy. But for preliminary reassurance, it should be stressed that for so volcanic an underpinning the S&P 500 futures index isn't much more volatile than our bread and butter OEX. But the volatility of the OEX is far more predictable and measured.

Other indexes technically similar to the OEX are the Technology Index on the Pacific Stock Exchange and the Amex Oil & Gas Index. Most are so thinly traded that they lack the essential basis of the OEX—its controlled volatility, or buying-selling pressures, and hence its profitability.

For example, on a day when the OEX had a total call open interest volume of 453,669 contracts, and a total put open interest volume of 495,017, the Technology Index had a total call open interest volume of 89 and a total put open interest volume of 19. A more favorable example on that day was the Major Market Index, which had a total call open interest volume of 68,312 and a put volume of 44,677. (Open interest is the number of contracts carried over to the next day. A contract is an agreement to buy or sell any financial instrument.)

We have said that the numbers in the OEX box that interest us are those surrounding the closing index, which, in this case, is the number 231.95. We are interested in these options because they contain the desired premiums, which will vary from about one to about three, give or take one-half to one. But below one the premium becomes too small, and above 3 1/2 it becomes too large. At $4 per contract very high profits beckon, but so do losses in some circumstances, namely, very volatile markets. There are usually plenty of options that meet our requirements, as we will begin to see in the next chapter. And if they aren't plentiful today, you have only to wait a day or two.

Market Timing

Market timing may be approached in two ways. You can buy market timing services or you can learn to do it yourself. A combination of the two is best, since you must become expert enough to trust your own judgment about any market decision you make in the course of trading. So, one should be familiar with the methods of Prechter and the others, adding your own approaches as you go along.

Note that long-term market timing appears not to be of special relevance in option trading since the economy is the factor in deciding where the market will be six months or a year hence. If the economy is healthy, the market will almost certainly be bullish; if not the market will be indecisive or bearish. Judgments about the economy thus seem a far cry from options trading with its instant pressures. But economists disagree. However, daily news about the economy often makes the market move convulsively, and thus decisively for options trading. A wise market timer will know everything about the economy. It doesn't mean that such a person must be an economist; perish the thought. It means that one must digest economic trends. Daily reading of appropriate journals will suffice.

If there is disagreement about long-term market prospects, obscurantism hovers over the short-term market. Short-term will be defined as anything going on this minute into the next two or three weeks. Part of this obscurantism is verbal.

Technical analysts are as guilty as fundamental analysts in generating the linguistic miasma that often pervades discourse in this field. Technical analysts, who argue that the market moves according to cycles and internal pressures having nothing to do with politics or the general economy, talk about volume, double bottoms, advance/decline ratios, the trading index (TRIN), the tick, and so forth. Fundamental analysts focus on the economy and on individual balance sheets of companies they follow and their relation to the economy.

Verbal categories of both types of analysts are accorded a kind of mystical force binding all who enter their realm, including the market itself, which is a participant, willy nilly.

Volume is the basis of much technical analysis, especially volume reversal, which occurs when a sudden surge of volume accompanies a market direction that then changes, up or down, less often sideways. Yet volume is nothing more than the sum total of investment decisions. Any self-respecting computer can report it. So highly successful a market analyst as Mark Leibovit bases all his analysis on volume and its reversal. In the old days, Joseph E. Granville was the volume expert. He stubbed his toe when the market went up and his analysis went down.

Double bottoms, triple, quadruple, depending on who is talking, are metaphorical adjuncts or constructs, as well as sight lines on charts. The doubling and tripling of a bottom, like the doubling and tripling of a floor or ceiling, are somehow supposed to add strength to the structure. Thus, who could doubt that a bear market, having lost 20 percent in a decline to Dow 800, as in 1982, would gird itself for a determined upward push from a ground floor that had a double bottom? It takes muscle to push up after the bear has been pushed down, and the double bottom, with the bear pawing listlessly, perhaps near expiration, is a sturdy support for the new animal surge, as the bear changes into a bull. But double bottoms are not more secure than no bottom, if the market goes "through the floor," as sometimes happens. Are we then to discard these concepts? No, but they are to be used in conjunction with other timing indicators.

"Support levels" are also tossed into the language hopper to show the price a stock will sell for at a top or bottom. Often a precise mathematical value is assigned, as a function of price-earnings (the last quarter or two), market value, or other considerations such as the volatility *(beta)* number in which 1.00 is average. If a stock happens to violate the support number, a new one is assigned.

It is a perfectly harmless game that will deceive nobody and profit few; there is something called momentum that will cancel out the best-laid support level. Momentum, not precisely a technical term, is a fact; when much buying or selling flows into a stock it will move more rapidly than any support figure can control. That is especially true in the case of a sudden play on a stock that may have been thinly traded, which is a characteristic of the greater number of OTC stocks and quite a few on the other exchanges. NYSE stocks are less likely to go through these gyrations unless they become takeover candidates or suffer a disaster. Momentum is simply the gathering of force or volume and the pressures up or down that ensue. It is a fact volume moves markets and a good market timer must be aware of it. Tracking volume requires a computer program or the burning of midnight oil to check volume numbers in the paper.

It should be noted that so unexceptional a principle as this, to which all market experts would nod in bored agreement, is far from infallible. For example, the volume increased for three consecutive days (July 7, 8, 9, 1987), to around 200 million shares, from levels of around 155 million shares the previous week. To true believers, this one included, the signal was clear enough; now is the time for all good speculators to come to the aid of their pocketbooks—and plunge. That would have been a mistake for some investors; the market acted like Morris the Cat in commercials. When presented with the wrong food the cat yawned. Many interpretations, mostly gloomy, followed this frightening episode, suggesting a consensus that the great bull market had ended at last. It didn't. But to OEX traders who bought bull spreads it could have been a sobering experience. To market timers, expecting an explosion upward, it might have been slightly embarrassing. The point is that no single point of reference on market timing is to be believed on its own, but all available, understandable signals should be checked. Greek oracles were similar omens. Nobody ever said investing was easy.

Something Happens

Stocks fall when something happens to earnings, earnings prospects, management quality and character, the competition, the timeliness of the product, long term use, demand and availability of the product, and all other related events inside and outside the company and its product. On a larger scale, market sectors go through similar phases, as did the entire computer industry between 1984 and 1986 or the precious metals industry between 1980 and 1986. Entire markets experience such shocks, only they are called recessions, in consequence of the malaise of various large sectors of the economy. Thus, autos and housing fell into a decline between August and November 1979, followed by other large segments of the economy. A minor upturn in 1980 interrupted the recession, which resumed in 1981 and deepened through much of 1982, when it ended dramatically to the snorting of the bull market.

Market timing that ignores large individual sectors of the economy will fail more often than not, for the market itself will not overlook such events.

Moving averages (high and low points) of each day's trading in the OEX and other indexes are a day-to-day graph based on the day's high and low numbers. Volume numbers are indispensable timing tools, whether or not you subscribe to the volume reversal theory or the on-balance volume theory of Granville. Volume is nothing more than concentrated buying or selling, and volume precedes price movement frequently. Steady-state volume usually signals a sideways market—the most common kind.

Moving averages produce charts of cycles—up and down behavior over time that translates into patterns. When a chart of such averages has jagged up and down movements, the stock or option is said to have high volatility and *beta* or rate of movement. Moving averages can be segmented into periods of any duration, from hours to decades. The idea of cycles in market behavior is both appealing and ridiculous. Their appeal is to the deepest human instincts. Everybody knows about biological cycles, the seasons, about famines in days of yore and in the modern Sahel in Africa, about activities associated with cycles, as love in spring, birth and death, women's menstrual cycles. Astrology has convinced people that cycles in their personal lives can be charted in accordance with real or imagined activities of planets which, presumably, have their own cycles, including the moon and earth's tides, and the sun and its cycles.

These phenomena affect people so they must affect markets. But how? Forgetting the food growth cycles that dictate these markets, or did before freezing, canning and other mass preservatives, it is difficult to believe that markets are preordained. Some people point to the increasing participation of women in markets and link market and menstrual cycles, noting that some women have temporary psychological and physical stresses during that period. But most women do not; stress is not the norm. One suspects that people who make this association have poor relationships with women. Market behavior may or may not cure that problem.

Market timing must get involved in cycles, if for no other reason than that influential market technicians chart them and make pronouncements that have influence.

Charts report what happened. Chartists then extrapolate from what has happened to what they think will happen. It takes little more than peasant cunning to know that trouble enters at this point. What has happened to the market does not necessarily imply what will happen, beyond superficial, lingering effects. When markets are very strong at the close of the day's trading, either up or down, a residual effect often occurs at the next opening (up or down), simply because all the orders may not have been executed. But that effect usually clears away rapidly.

Charts are a kind of deception; they make it appear as if they actually foretell what they report. Rarely does a chartist remind you that charts are after the fact, like box scores in baseball games. The baseball expert is not fooled by box scores; he knows that because Frank Thomas hits two home runs on Tuesday that he won't necessarily hit two more on Wednesday. He knows that Thomas has the same ability to do so, but many factors are unknown and relate to his potential on the day following the box score. If you ask Thomas he will say something like "It depends on who's pitching," and if you chart the Thomas performance you will indeed see that if his home runs come most frequently against certain kinds of pitching, the absence of that type may well decrease his home run production. But notice; that is *fundamental analysis.* It is real world data, even if it hasn't happened yet—the next pitcher may not yet be announced, though speculation can narrow the field. Even so, the next pitcher weighs more heavily on the Thomas performance—his "moving averages"—than do the averages themselves. That is where the market analysis breaks down. It cannot take into account all the relevant real world events now happening and yet to happen that affect market performance. Nor can it take into account all the relevant internal market events. Not all can be known.

Nevertheless, anyone betting on home run hitters will bet on Thomas rather than on a player who rarely hits home runs. A market that is going up is favored by the odds to continue doing that. If the OEX is advancing Monday, Tuesday and Wednesday, however, it does not follow that it will advance on Thursday. Contrary opinion enters here to the effect that if everyone knows something or expects something, it is wrong or won't occur. Many people would say that contrary opinion is nothing more than simple orneriness, but they would be wrong. Markets do turn around when sentiment seems to favor it the least. They turn up when everybody is bearish or down when the contrary mood prevails. There are reasons: when everybody is bearish it means simply that all selling has been done, and when everybody is bullish no one is doing any more buying—everybody is all bought out.

So a market timer must be aware constantly of what chartists are saying, especially when they report degrees of bullishness or bearishness.

Note that there is no real disagreement between many fundamental and technical analysts; it is a matter of emphasis. Technicians do talk about real world events, as in the effects of Federal Reserve Board actions, interest rates, business statistics, citing these factors to interpret their own numbers. Statistics are like that well-known lamppost; you lean against it for support or use it for illumination. Statistics are not in themselves deceptive, but our interpretations are something else.

Cycle theories appeal to many basic instincts. Their appeal is mystical as well, because they appeal to our sense of history. The most famous of these theories is the Kondratieff Wave, which posits recurring depressions every fifty years. Depressions come along often enough—at least the recession version of them—to make people look hard at Kondratieff. Stalin considered him a menace to dialectical materialism and murdered him, as any primitive chief would do to the bearer of bad news. What should we think of him?

If the last major depression is identified as the 1929 giant, the wave is well overdue. But since that depression didn't actually end until war spending took over in the late 1930s, a depression soon would make Kondratieff only off by a year or two. Earlier periods offer inconclusive data. Because society changes so fundamentally over long periods of time, especially as regards to the economy itself and what its leading elements consist of at any point in history, it is more or less pointless to base behavior on decades-old data. Any cycle theory, however, is based on a kind of fatalism, a view of human history that says we are more or less powerless to alter it. That's the real problem with any cycle theory.

There is, to be sure, a sense in which humanity is indeed powerless to alter behavior, both human and natural. Cycles, such as life and death, winter and summer, hunger and satiety, sex and birth, cannot be changed, though some of their extremes can be altered. You can move to a climate without winter. Human life can be increased slightly by means of modern medicine. Sex and birth can be interrupted in various ways for various ends. Environment can be altered drastically, including obliteration via nuclear war.

But depressions are largely failures of economic relations. Are these relations biological, environmental, theological? Environment includes nature, which permits some alterations, but it also includes what we loosely call sociological environments. These include economic relations, and here humanity has shown that it can alter at will, depending on the social contract that is chosen. If we choose to control the economy centrally, as in communism or facism or via individual business and commercial decisions, as in capitalism, we make certain kinds of differing economic behavior more or less inevitable. Some features of economics appear impervious to alteration—the land will only support X number of people before impoverishment of both land and people sets in. This seems true even when you add technology. Japan and Korea prove merely that technology can overcome natural shortcomings only by exporting the poverty. Japanese technological and marketing genius extracted market share from other countries that proved less aggressive in marketing or less fortunate in currency fluctuation. The effects were to transfer Japanese (and Korean, Chinese, etc.) poverty to the United States and Europe. Undoubtedly this will change, without affecting the argument.

Meanwhile, back at the ranch, as the Western movies had it, the option trader awaits timing advice. The point is that cycle theories should be consulted, despite the questions raised above, and one should keep a record of one's own investments in light of cycle theories and other timing indicators. Cycle theories are at the heart of much technical analysis; they cannot be ignored In the short term, they are less urgent than the indicators that relate to daily market behavior. But cycles apply even here, with many patterns apparently repeating themselves and affecting the OEX and all other options and equities. I refer to such phenomena as the "Monday blues," in which it is common for the market to decline on Mondays over several weeks in sequence. The market during each trading day often follows patterns of discernible behavior, as when it reverses from the opening direction, often around lunch time, raising questions of the relationship between gastronomy and finance.

More to the point, when trading the OEX there is little time to contemplate theories of timing. If birds studied flight they would not leave the ground. One must concentrate on the "gut issues," which include first of all, perhaps, the trading index or TRIN (it is called the ARMS index at the Financial News Network, after the last name of its inventor).

The TRIN measures the constant ebb and flow of buying and selling throughout the day, reflecting the preponderance of buying or selling. It is measured numerically by upticks versus downticks (buys and sells). When they are about equal in number, the TRIN is 1.00. As the balance tips the number reflects market direction. If the market goes up the number goes down and vice versa. But it is market direction that is all-important and the TRIN can be in bear market territory, around 1.25, for example, and turn around suddenly, taking the OEX and the S&P 500 futures with it. A strong upward movement can commence, turning the market around even though the Dow may be down in negative territory, and the advance/decline ratio (number of stocks advancing versus number declining) can be in favor of the losers.

The TRIN reflects what is going on among the big actors of the NYSE drama; just as IBM and General Motors can have a crucial effect on the market as a whole, so they and their fellow big capitalization stocks can move the stock indexes and futures around in midstream, turning bear into bull and bull into bear.

The TRIN is also a longer-term market indicator, and if a record of it is kept day after day (as some computer programs do) it can be a highly useful timing help—and not just for the moment.

The advance/decline ratio is another vital timing device for short-term trading. The OEX responds closely to it, perhaps more closely than does the Dow, which sometimes conflicts. If more stocks are advancing than declining it is probable that the OEX will be in plus territory as well, but it is not inevitable. If several of the big stocks in the OEX—say IBM and GM—decline while the preponderance of stocks advance, the OEX will be held back. In such a case, however, the Dow will also be restrained.

The OEX and the Dow move closely in parallel, but not quite hand in glove. For purposes of trading, and timing as well, one always looks to the Dow as well as the transportation and utilities averages for clues.

Other timing indicators include news from the other markets, including the AMEX and OTC. It is well to look at financial futures markets, especially the S&P 500 futures. The put-call ratio is important, as are cycle charts of three-day, ten-day and other moving averages. When all these internally generated numbers are moving together, along with the Dow components, the TRIN, the tick (upticks and downticks are instantaneous counts of buys and sells), and all the other indicators above, it is still important to know what's going on in the outside world.

The fundamentals of the economy and world politics

intrude on markets constantly. The United States issues a stream of statistics, such as the leading indicators, the money supply, unemployment numbers, that often have immediate and violent impact on market timing.

Thus we see the problems that arise in getting a precise handle on market timing. There is first the language problem in which the market is treated metaphorically and in which colorful language conceals emotive force that can be misleading. Then there is the conflicting data that flows in constantly, and the ease with which false inferences may be drawn from data. It is sobering but not fatal to try to sort out what can be believed, and that is what we are trying to do. But it can only be done within the context of trading, with all its chaos and uncertainty. Financial markets are not exactly like fish markets, but they are not leisurely, outdoor art shows either.

Each trade in this book called upon a selective list of timing devices, simply because they appeared to be relevant. When the market opens on huge volume, with the advance/decline ratio overwhelmingly up or down, with the TRIN at .25 or 2.00, with the tick showing almost total buying or selling, with the Dow rising or dropping rapidly and being confirmed by the OEX, with the other stock option indexes such as the Major Market Index moving in tandem, and with no letup in these moves after the first hour, one needs no further timing indicators. Virtually everything you need to know is in this paragraph. But such days occur only six or eight times a year —perhaps a few more in the years to come.

It is the ordinary trading day, when nothing galvanic happens, that the fine-tuning of timing indicators enters the fray. After a long move in the Dow, up or down, the question of tops and bottoms enters front and center. Then such things as head and shoulder formations and inverted head and shoulder formations—which are simply chart patterns creating these mnemonic devices—may be useful. They may, indeed, be decisive. At other times they may be irrelevant, as with any other single timing indicator.

After the market has been trading back and forth over an extended period, with no unusual fluctuations in volume, the wise OEX trader will watch volume figures carefully. Sudden changes in volume can lead to a new market environment requiring a change in tactics. Considerations of this sort affect all other timing devices.

C H A P T E R 3

Strategy One:
Vertical Spreads

Our first strategy requires for its best effect a trendless market, in which great splurges up or down do not occur. In a word, boring. You may inquire testily when such a market exists. Most obviously it exists once the crisis is past, when the market has done its worst or best. Often worst and best go together for the option trader. The 1987 October crash of 508 points was followed by a quick recovery of about 300 points, and then a slow, back and forth regrouping to new highs.

That slow, back and forth recovery was the ideal time for Strategy One (and for Strategy Three, the selling of both sides of a combination). More recent markets, following the October 13, 1989, mini-massacre of 190 points, were equally congenial for this strategy, as we will see.

The October 1989 drop of 190 points had been preceded by three days of rising volume and declining prices. Volume almost always goes up when the market makes big moves in either direction. At such a point it is reckless to put on a spread unless you use both bull and bear spreads. Faced with rising volume, you know that the market is going to make an emphatic move. If you cannot decide the direction based solely on volume, you must seek other indicators.

Throughout the summer of 1989 the market had been rocking along in a fairly narrow trading range, after a sharp correction down to 2420 in June. It recovered steadily up to 2620 and traded more or less in a range of about 100 points until the end of September, when a rally up to new all-time highs took hold, carrying the Dow up to about 2820. It collapsed in five downward days, culminating in the debacle of October 13.

A sharp recovery back to 2700 was followed by a steadier course. From mid-November to mid-December the market invited the use of spreads.

The spread strategy we now address is of very low risk, making it appropriate for people with speculative cash and instincts. You do not need "riverboat gambler" instincts (Robert Kennedy's description of Lyndon B. Johnson); the occasional purchase of a lottery ticket or the vacation pulling of a Las Vegas slot machine will qualify you. Your bank account will reveal whether you qualify financially. You need only $5,000 to open an account for five sets of calls and puts. But you also need to develop market smarts, which are a cross between intuition and daily study of the market in all its aspects. The OEX does not move in a vacuum.

What we do here is to hedge against violent movements and crisis. You own puts if the market drops dramatically; you own calls if it goes up in the same fashion. The overall point is to make profits while avoiding excessive risk in the process.

You buy and sell puts below the OEX level and you buy and sell calls above the same OEX level. You can use an interval between 15 and 25 OEX points between the strike prices of the two options you sell. Closer intervals are risky. Like the quarterback driven out of the "pocket," you may have to scramble to regain the play's intent.

The mechanics of these transactions are that you sell the higher priced call and buy the lower priced; you sell the higher priced put and buy the lower priced. That gives you a profit on both sides of the spread. It is called "out-of-the-money vertical selling" in some quarters. It is also called a bear call spread and a bull put spread or just plain spreading.

Obviously if the market breaks out of the trading range interval, up or down, you will lose small amounts of money, unless you move to repair the damage. It isn't always possible but the extent of the loss, if the market drops, is the difference between the put you bought and the put you sell at the time you decide to leave the trade. Part of the loss will be made up by the profit on the calls. If the market goes up beyond the trading range the same situation prevails.

Taking the Plunge

I once heard a well-known commodities trader say that anyone wanting to learn the trade should be prepared to lose $10,000. It was a kind of entrance fee. Trading options of any kind creates losses. By spreading and counter-balancing, you can minimize losses, as we will see.

For the first example, we picked a spread as follows, when the OEX was at 323. (The OEX is much higher than that today, but the relationships change very little.)

The calls: sold five 335s for 2 3/16 each, bought five 340s for 1 1/16 each, or in dollars, sold five 335s for $218.75 each. We sold five contracts and bought five. For selling, we took in $1093.75. For buying, we paid $530 ($106 × 5).

The puts: sold 305 puts for 2 1/4 each, bought five 300 puts for 1 13/16 each. For selling we took in $1125 ($275 × 5). For buying, we paid $905 ($181 × 5).

From selling the calls and subtracting those we bought, we received $563.75. Selling the puts and subtracting those we bought comes to $220. Adding these two produces $783.75.

None of this includes commissions, which vary from broker to broker, but would be several hundred dollars in some cases.

The trade was uneventful during the first week, which is exactly what you seek. We want these relationships to remain more or less in a steady state so as to expire worthless—as time goes on options melt down—so that we profit to the tune of $783 or thereabouts. We got nervous at the end of the month, worrying about a New Year's rally (this was in December). We decided to clear out of the trade. That means you have to buy back what you sold and sell what you bought. The market had moved the OEX from 323 to 329, closing in on 335, the danger point. Though commission costs were over $100, which put the trade into a small loss, the trade itself actually wound up with a profit of $64. The moral of this trade: we entered it too early in the cycle. You want to enter a trade as close to the end of the cycle as possible and consistent with worthwhile price levels. This trade had the price levels but not the time. Remember the Browning linc "ncver the time, the place, the girl together . . ." Remember the date, the price level and the profit together, for those who would romance the petulant options market.

The question of when to begin a new spread is one that should be made with great caution or automatically, depending on two things—your psychology of investing and the condition of the market. If you like to agonize over decisions about money, please feel free. Agony is akin to ecstasy in some circumstances—in book titles, overeating, etc.—and it may be instructive as to investing procedure, for money does not come easily and it is well to avoid encouraging an easy departure for it.

Market condition hardly needs to be stressed. But plenty of market technicians say that fundamentals about the market and the economy it reflects should not be taken into account. But this is like saying only the bathing suit, not the girl, should be taken into account. One should learn as much as possible on the assumption that while a little learning is indeed a dangerous thing, a lot of learning may at least be reassuring even if it turns out to be not more instructive. To go to your defeat knowing a great deal shows at least that you do not take defeat lightly. It might even cause you to resolve to win. That may explain the next trade. On January 3, with options expiration eleven days away I entered a new trade. The market had leaped up on the first two trading days, with increasing volume. The "January effect," in which the market more often than not rises in the first week, appeared in place.

The OEX was at 335, and with expiration less than two weeks away, returns weren't very enticing. Note that in the first trade the options were at a comfortable distance from each other, with 40 points on the buying side, 30 points on the selling side.

The calls: sold five 345s for 1 1/8 each, bought five 350 calls for 1/2. In dollars, the sale was $113 × 5 or $565, the buying of five calls for $50, or $50 × 5, cost $250. Subtracting the $250 from $565 netted $315.

The puts: sold five puts for 1 11/16, or in dollars, $168.75 × 5, or $843.75. Bought five puts for $106.25 × 5, or $531.25. Subtracting the puts you buy from the puts you sell gives you $312.50. Adding this number to the calls gives you $312.50 plus $315, or a total of $627.50 (minus commission).

To go with this spread, and because the market wasn't moving very much, we decided to add another spread. Sometimes there is safety in numbers.

This time, because of the nearness to expiration—only three days away—premiums were very low. We doubled the number of sales from five to ten. This required doubling our margin account.

The calls: sold ten 325s for 7/16 each, bought five 330s for 1/8 cach. In dollars, the sale was $437.50 for the 325s (7/16 cquals .4375 or $43.75 each); the cost of the five 330s at 1/8 was $62.50.

Subtracting the cost side from the sell side yields $375.00.

On the put side; sold ten 305s for 7/16, bought five 330s for 1/8. The sale brought in $437.50 or ten × $43.75. The cost of buying five 330s was $12.50 × 5 or $62.50. That meant a profit of $375, in other words the same as the call side. Adding them together meant $750, minus commission.

The simple act of doubling the sell side exposed that side to a doubling or more of the risk, since only half the calls were hedged by purchasing offsetting calls. Adding to that the doubling of margin costs means that more money was riding on the outcome. But time was short and as it turned out sweet enough. At expiration the totals were a profit of $750, minus a commission of several hundred. It isn't much, but you can always double and quadruple the number of contracts once you get the hang of it.

Note that margin requirements can be covered by stocks and bonds. So you need a general account with an option eligibility.

The time was January 8, 1990. We owned a bear spread (more later) on the theory that the market was going to respond to the worldwide symptoms starting in Japan. There the market was declared, finally, to be overpriced. This charge had been made for years based on price-earnings ratios of 60 compared with our 13 or 14. Of course everybody knew that the Japanese financial structure differed from ours. Japan had most of the world's biggest banks and bank accounts which were busily engaged in achieving what the Imperial Japanese Army and Navy attempted ingloriously in earlier times—to take over the world, peacefully this time. The U.S. market, which could have been pardoned for cheering at the news of Japan's first defeat in decades, reacted nervously.

My own view is that Japan bashing is irrational; the Japanese are successful because they have applied U.S. methods, now long out of style here, to their own procedures. We now need to copy them.

Calls: we sold ten Jan 325s for 7/16—a clear sign that the market was betting on a bear move, offering so thin a premium —and bought five 330s for 1/8.

Puts: we sold ten Jan 305s for 1; we bought five 300s for 5/8. The main reason for the low premiums, apart from bearish sentiment, was the proximity of options expiration on January 19. Note that we raised the ante—five extra puts and calls were sold otherwise the trade wasn't worth doing. The totals: maximum profit was $1,065. Potential for loss was increased since we weren't hedging (buying puts and calls) as much as we were selling. The ten 325s at 7/16 or $43.75 brought in $437; the ten Jan 305 puts brought in $1,000 for a $1,437 total. Subtracting the calls we bought, five at 1/8 or $60, and the five 300 puts we bought for 5/8 or $62.50 × 5 equaling $312.50, brought down the total take to $1065 if all went according to Rosy Scenario.

The market, indifferent to our analysis that it was in for calamity, rose sharply January 16. The 305 puts were now at 7/16 down from 1; the five 300 puts we bought for 5/8 were down to 3/16. The calls: the 325s we sold for 7/16 were up to 11/16 and the 300s we bought for 1/8 were at 1/4.

The pull downward of a short remaining time period was greater than the push upward of market forces. We were ahead of the game. On the next day the market lost all it had gained the day before. The OEX closed at about 317, a mere point away from our initial position. The ten Jan 325 calls we sold for 7/16 were at 1/4; the five 330s we bought for 1/8 were at 1/16. The puts: the ten 305s we bought for 1 were now at 9/16, the five 300s we bought for 5/8 were now at 3/8. We had a good profit now, but decided to roll the dice the day before expiration date. The market heeded our pleas for mercy and closed about where it began, not before giving us a slight case of terminal stage fright, as it rose strongly in the morning taking the OEX up with it 2 1/2 points. But it beat a retreat from there, calling it a day around 317.

The trade worked perfectly with both ends expiring worthless, earning us the full amount, $1,065 minus commissions.

The three trades we have done, which were spread over thirteen trading days, permit several inferences. All were brief trades, of several day's duration. Only one of them had any degree of risk, the last one in which we added five calls and five puts for a total of ten each instead of the usual five. The strategy paid off rapidly. It also required $5,000 of added margin (in stocks and bonds).

Financial and economic analysis is both art and science; as science it is mostly inexact, on the order of psychology and history, not on the order of physics or chemistry. As art it relies on the intuitive response to data. If you see the market going down but believe in contrary indicators that you feel are insufficiently factored into market selling, you will move accordingly and oppositely in your trading. However, history does not reveal whether "Mary, Mary, quite contrary" was a successful options player.

Because OEX trading moves so quickly you must watch the market carefully and constantly, or have a broker who does and who carries out your program. But you may have to do the entire program yourself, using a large discount broker with a proven ability at trading the OEX. It also means that if you decide to go in for OEX trading systematically, using many contracts, say 20 to 100 or more, you can expect to become a full time options trader. You can do it at home, with a computer and modem or, more modestly, with the Financial News Network. Its ticker tape is electronic and fifteen minutes late, by law. But it works, and you also get commentary that is both valuable and informed. Both the resident experts and those outside FNN give you much of the background information you need know about general market conditions. You also need the *Wall Street Journal* and/or *Investor's Daily.*

New Trade, New Time

Let us come forward in time, to 1994, to test whether vertical spreads using the OEX remain profitable.

Remember that vertical spreads are good only in a market that is bracketed into a fairly narrow range—as most markets are for much of the time. When volatility sets in you must go to bull and bear spreads, combinations, and other tactics.

In early March 1994, the OEX was trading around 430. Since our last OEX trading took place in 1990 when strike prices were around 330 you can see how kindly the years treat vertical spreading. It took four years to move up 100 OEX points. But of course there were large moves in those four years, and anyone using only vertical spreads throughout the time would have had to be very nimble indeed. When the Dow made a low of around 3550 in September 1993, the OEX dropped below 400. When the Dow threatened 4000 in January 1994 and again in September 1994, the OEX followed dutifully along, moving into the 440s and above, briefly. These four-year moves show that despite all the scary features of OEX trading, there is a core of predictability about it, namely that however rapidly it may move within a 24 hour period, the moves tend to flatten out as time marches on. Perhaps my advice to watch the OEX throughout the day when you get involved in it is bad counsel. The less you watch, the better you might be. But that is something for each person to decide. It has to do with risk tolerance and pressure and the way you react. OEX trading requires you to be cool under fire.

In early March 1994, you could have put on a vertical spread.

The OEX was at 431.71. Only 12 trading days remained so premiums were thin. You need 10 contracts, as follows:

Calls; sell 440 at 1 3/8, or 10 × 137.50 equals $1,375.00. Buy the 445s at 1/2, or 10 × 50 equals $500. Subtract the cost of $500 from the sale of $1,375.00, and you gain $875.

Puts; sell 410s at 3/4, or 10 × $75 equals $750. Buy the 400s at 1/2, or 10 × 50 equals $500. Subtract cost of $500 from the sale of $750 and you gain $250. Add gain from calls of $875 giving a total gain of $1125.

Sparing you the details, the OEX traded within a narrow range for the next 12 trading days; the options expired and the entire profit was in the bank (minus commissions). There was a sharp drop for a few days, warming up the 410 puts, but the trade was unscathed. An argument for NOT watching the tape constantly appeared one day when it seemed that the market would drop down to the 410 mark. It didn't.

The market collapse from over 3900 to near 3500 in March had stabilized more or less in April and May, trading mostly between 3650 and 3750. That kind of range favors vertical spreading.

Around the beginning of June a spread as follows, with the OEX at 424, looked good enough in an otherwise dull period. Calls: sell 430s at 1 5/16, or 10 × 131.25 equals $1,312.50. Buy the 435s at 7/16 or 10 × 43.75 equals $437.50. Subtract the cost of 437.50 from the sale of 1,312.50, and you gain $875.

Puts: sell the 405s at 13/16 or 10 × 81.25 equals $812.50. Buy the 400s at 9/16 or 10 × 56.25 equals $562.50. Subtract the cost of 562.50 from the sale of 812.50, and you gain $250. Add gain from calls of $875 giving a total of $1,125.

This was like catching fish in a barrel; the market barely moved through the expiration period. Gains were $1,125, minus commissions. One observer said the market is "wandering around in a little corral." That's what the OEX doctor ordered.

A vertical spread in July and/or August also would have produced the same results, more or less, as in June. July was a difficult month for vertical spreads; bull spreads and buying OEX calls outright would have paid off. The market began a sharp rise August 20 that carried it through the next week and a half. Here too a vertical spread would have failed.

Beginning in September the climate was right again, once past the attempt to make a new high around 4000. It failed and the market dropped quickly back into another trading range. The market dropped taking the OEX from the low 440s to the low 430s. When markets spurt up and down, as they do increasingly in response to program trading, it is a sign that a trading range is at hand. Program trading is cut off by the collars at 50 Dow points up or down. The individuals calling the shots have differing trading goals that differ from yours. Most big fund managers, whose buying and selling can cause the program trading to erupt, also have different trading goals, though mostly they have a lot of money that needs to be invested in favored areas of the market. These differing interests are what make the market move, until suddenly the public gets interested. That puts another force into the equation. There is no one guiding hand, whether visible or invisible, but if I had to pick one it would be the hands of the big fund managers. Now if we only knew what such hands had in mind.

We waited out most of September, not wanting to be trapped too early in the next expiration date in October (third Friday). Twenty trading days stretched ahead when the following trade was begun.

Calls: sell 440s at 1 1/8 or 10 × 112.50 equals $1,125. Buy 445s at 1/2 or 10 × 50 equals $500. Subtract the cost of $500 from the sale of $1,125, and you have a gain of $625.

Puts: sell Oct 405s at 1 3/16 or 10 × 118.75 equals $1187.50. Buy 400s at 7/8 or 10 × 87.50 equals $875. Subtract the cost of 875 from 1187.50 and you gain 312.50. The total: $937.50.

As you can see, the OEX was at the same level as in the previous trade in June, but the numbers were different as the time was in relation to expiration—shorter in June. I judged, therefore, that there was more pressure on the downside of the market, since the puts were richer though the time was longer than in the earlier (June) trade.

A week later the OEX was trading about 4 points lower. It wobbled back and forth until it resumed its advance, closing in on our 440 calls. But it calmed down and the options expired giving up the $937 total (minus commissions).

Strategy Two:
Bull and Bear Spreads

Spreads

A spread demands that you pay attention to market movement as the first consideration, not market inaction that you hope for in combinations. In this it resembles our hopes when we buy options—market movement is crucial there, too.

But market direction is also a key to spreads. If we believe the market is going up we plan on a bull spread, if down we do a bear spread. Obviously the spread tactic puts us instantly into market timing in the near-term and intermediate aspects. It should always be undertaken in a market that moves emphatically.

Because spreads are profitable only in general market movements, you may wonder how they differ from simple buying of options or buying of option spreads. With individual options you need a far bigger move in the market to double your money than you need for the spread. A move of about 45 Dow points, which is not uncommon these days, has been known to double your money in a spread but not with individual options unless something unique to that option occurs. There is also far more risk in buying individual options than spreads. With spreads, losses should never be more than 1/3 to 1/2, in frequency and extent. The frequency of risk in individual option buying is between 70 and 80 percent as noted. The extent can be controlled, of course, but risk is certainly greater.

If risks in spreads are limited, so are profits. The procedure for spreading is that you buy an in-the-money OEX option with the strike price closest to the current OEX index level, and you sell the out-of-the-money option with the strike price closest to the same index level. Both options should also have the same expiration. If you think the market is going up, you put on a bull spread using calls. If you think it's going down, you use puts in a bearish spread. You should never pay more than $2.50 ($250 per contract) for a spread, otherwise it's not worth doing. Basically it's because money is made when the spread widens, which it will do if the market moves up in the case of the bull spread or down with the bear spread. But the spread can't widen more than $5, which is the difference between the two strike prices—the one you bought and the one you sold.

So long as you pay no more than $2.50 for the spread you will have the possibility of making $2.50 or 100 percent in profit. The same $2.50 will always be the worst possible loss, though you should never allow it to go that far.

You must look for the highest premium possible in the operation you sell. It should never be less than $2 for an out-of-the-money OEX put and not less than $2.50 for an OEX call. An out-of-the-money option premium is time value entirely, and the more you can get for selling time, the more likely you are to come out a winner. Time will pass, no matter what else the market does. Some experts believe that high option premiums on calls indicate an upward market bias, just as such premiums on puts are a prelude to a declining market. It doesn't always work that way.

The spread strategy does work because the in-the-money-calls gain more quickly than the out-of-the-money calls, when the market goes up, thus widening the spread. Exactly similar movements occur with puts; when the market declines the in-the-money-puts appreciate more rapidly than out-of-the-money puts, again widening the spread. When the market moves sufficiently to push both call or put options into-the-money, the spread will widen as time goes on until the two options will be exactly 5 points apart. That is the maximum profit possible. But if the market moves against you, pushing both options out-of-the-money, the spread will narrow. At expiration they could become worthless.

The Trading

Let's begin with a real life trade. In the middle of August 1986, the OEX index was at 237. It had moved up in a market surge

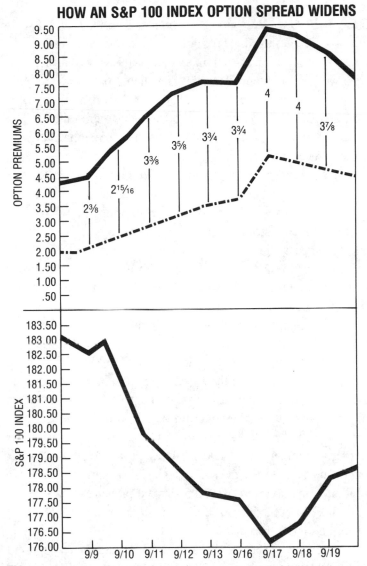

HOW AN S&P 100 INDEX OPTION SPREAD WIDENS

This graph shows the actual premium movements of a bearish spread initiated on September 9, 1985, with November 180 and 185 S&P 100 Index options. Notice how the spread, opened at 2-3/8, widened to 4 as the Index declined from 182.58 to 176.09.

to the 1860 Dow level, about 60 points from its July 1 low. It appeared to be heading for higher levels, at least sufficiently higher for our purposes—a bull spread. Later we will discuss the signs we used to support a bull rather than a bear spread at this point. We bought the Oct 235 call at $7.00 or $700 per contract, and we sold the 240 call for $4.50 or $450 per contract. The spread cost $2.50 (subtract $4.50 from $7), meaning that with five contracts your cost is 12 1/2 points or $1,250.

We will discover that our maximum profit is the same $1,250 and so is the maximum loss, because the spread can never widen beyond 5 points. One exception: the difference between the two strike prices in some markets.

If the cost and profit are the same the risk/reward ratio is 1 to 1. That doesn't sound too remarkable until you compare the results and the risk/reward with simply buying options. The same purchase outright (no spread) would give you a debit of $2,200 if you bought five of the 240 calls at $4.50; the debit would be $3,500 if you bought five of the 235 calls at $7.00. Moreover, it happens on occasions that a move in the Dow of 40–45 points will widen the spread to 5 points, resulting in the doubling of your money. But the market usually has to make a major move in the right direction before you can expect such a result with mere buying of options, whether OEX or other kinds. Remember that it takes 7 Dow points to move 1 OEX point, and sometimes the OEX lags. Also, spread losses are smaller. The maximum is $1,250 in the present spread versus either $2,200 or $3,500. Of course, you never have to take total losses on any option position.

When any spread position begins to go against you, don't wait until losses mount. If the spread narrows from the original 2 1/2 to 1 3/4, it is time to abandon it, selling back the call you bought, buying back the call you sold, restricting your loss to $875.00. (Five contracts times 1 3/4.)

It is the selling of the lower-priced option that keeps your costs (and losses) down as compared with buying options. This also makes elimination of margin possible.

The spread we put on in the middle of August 1986, turned out to be a quick winner. By the third week in August it widened to the desired spread of 5. We doubled our money in a week, from $1,250 debit (the initial cost) to $2,500 credit. In other words, the 5 points ($500 per contract) times five contracts gave us a profit of $2,500 based on the initial cost of $1,250 or 100 percent profit with a margin cost (but it's our money, earning interest at the broker's) of about $5,000. The Dow moved rapidly from around 1820 to around 1900, cooperating completely.

What is meant by "the desired spread of 5?" Five points or $500 is the widest possible margin in spreads because the OEX is calibrated in strike prices 5 points apart. When the OEX index moves below the strike price of the lower call in your spread, both calls become worthless. When the OEX index moves above the strike price of the upper call in your spread, both calls have value but profits in the call you bought will be offset by losses in the call you sold as the spread goes above 5 points. So the maximum profit is always the difference between the strike price of the call you bought and the call you sold, minus the cost of the spread, initially. Identical calculations apply to a bear spread.

So, the less you have to pay for a spread the better. While trading you will see that we had a few trades less than the 2 1/2 point spread, but most of them were at that level, which is fine. Just don't pay more.

Other Spreads

Not all trades work so quickly and smoothly. Emboldened by so quick a gain, we next went into the spread market September 26, 1986, and discovered an alternate route to yet another kind of successful trade. But it was touchy, as in touch and go.

The OEX was at 223 (this was ten days after the 120 point Dow drop) and it seemed that the market would be in the mood for a sufficient resumption of the upward swing (actually a trading range swing) that had been so rudely interrupted by the detonations of September 11 and 12. We looked at the Oct 220 OEX for 6 1/4 and the Oct 225 for 3 5/8, but they didn't qualify—the price was not right. Remember, we said you needed to pay no more than $2.50 ($250 per contract) to come out ahead, and the prices we were looking at were higher. Was the market saying something? What about a bear spread using puts? The nearest in-the-money put was the Oct 225 at 5 1/2, the nearest out-of-the-money was Oct 220 at 3. That was 2 1/2!

Puts were it; we put on a bear spread, instead of a bull spread with calls. So we bought the Oct 225 put at 5 1/2, bought five contracts, that is, and we sold the Oct 220 put at 3, also times five. So, on September 22, we entered a bear spread, the contrary to the bull spread, paying $1,250 (5 1/2 × 5 equals $2,750 minus 3 × 5 or $1,500, which equals $1,250).

The next two days saw no change, but on September 25 there was rumbling; the Oct 220 was at 5 3/4, the Oct 225 at 8 3/4. The spread had gone from 2 1/2 to 3, favoring our contracts. The next day saw the spread expanding to 3 1/2. On September 29—our first week—the 225 was at 9, the 220 at 5 1/2, the spread 3 1/2. The market was dropping, but not sharply, and then shortly before noon the spread had widened to slightly over 4. We took it, buying back the put we had sold, selling the put we had bought. It was a good thing to do. We made a profit of $810.00, on a investment of $1,250 margin, in a week. Had we waited, when the market turned up sharply, we would have lost money, at least initially.

The next day, September 30, presented us with a tempting bull spread opportunity, in light of our total success so far. The market had been moving between 1740 and 1780, but the bias seemed upward, or so the OEX was telling us, offering a better price on a bull spread than on a new bear spread. But it was not quite $2.50, our essential and target price. We waited. It is important not to gain too much confidence in this kind of trading, or as the old saying has it "pride goeth before a fall." Once you think you have a foolproof system of trading options you had best give it up; you will certainly lose. There is no foolproof system, only a lowering of the odds and the acquisition of skills in reading market signals. The signal the market was giving us on the new bull spread was that it was unwilling to meet us halfway—it wasn't quite $2.50, which is halfway. It also happens to be the essential half; remember, you must never put on a bull spread that costs more than $2.50. If you can't do it today there is always tomorrow. The market will cooperate in a day or so; it wants your business.

On that philosophy, we waited, but not for long. On October 1, 1986, the right price arrived. The OEX closed at 221.59, gaining almost 2 points for the day. We bought the nearest in-the-money call, the Oct 220 at 4 7/8; we sold the nearest out-of-the-money call, the Oct 225 at 2 1/2. Our total cost was, therefore, 2 3/8, or 1/8 better than the 2 1/2 limit. If the market gave us an opportunity to take profit on the completed widened spread, we would thus gain 1/8 more. It isn't a bonanza, but, multiplied five or ten times, it pays commissions. If you do it often enough, it becomes very much worth doing. It's also an incentive to keep looking for the right price.

One should note that the history of spreads differs greatly from the history of combinations, where the decay of time value is the crucial issue. With spreads, time value has little impact. You await market movement. It didn't happen at first with the new bull spread. But there was no bad news either. The market moved fretfully for a week or so, then moved tantalizingly, flirting with the desired 5 point spread range. To make a somewhat lengthy story short, the right spread didn't occur until November 3, with the OEX at 231.95, or almost

232. The Dow was at 1894. It thus required a move of almost 10 OEX points (from 221.59 to 231.95) and a move in the Dow from around 1800 to around 1900. The time required to gain 100 percent of the original investment was just over a month. The movement was farther than necessary with the earlier bull spread. A move of 100 Dow points should translate into an OEX move of 14 points, according to the formula of 1 OEX point for every 7 of the Dow. As you can see, it doesn't always follow the formula, for the reasons we have noted—both the Dow and the OEX are weighted indices and heavyweights like IBM or GM can skew the formula. Sometimes this behavior can be very friendly, when a Dow move of a mere 40–45 points will cause the spread to widen sufficiently to give us the desired minimum profit of 4 or 4 1/2 points.

Nevertheless, our gain was 100 percent in about a month. If you add that to our bear spread and to the combinations we were also playing at that time, the results are impressive. Add the S&P 500 stock index futures for the big calamity days of September 11 and 12, and you are well on your way to your first million.

The Way to Go

Our success on November 3 inevitably made us conclude that spreads were the way to go—that the market was not in a real trading range but was sufficiently volatile to make spreads profitable. After all, even in a trading range market a move of 45 or 50 points can make a spread profitable, if you get the direction right. It's a big if, of course.

The next three trading days had little movement, hence no temptation for spreads. Because spreads require market movement, while combinations do not, and it is often profitable to trade both instruments simultaneously, it is necessary to have these two opposing ideas in one's head simultaneously. Scott Fitzgerald considered this the mark of highest intelligence; it is indispensable for success in options whether intelligent or not. But even the most demented Marxist dictator now regards profitability as a *sine qua non,* and we do not argue with such people.

Volume declined from 180 million shares November 3 to 120 or less November 10 and 11. It jumped to 160 on November 12, the signal we awaited. The OEX index was around 232 when we decided on a spread, but was it to be bull or bear? Volume had picked up only one day, and our theory is that you should wait a couple of days at least to discern the way of the wind. It is vital to wait a few days before doing combinations because you look for a trendless spell, and a single day does not constitute a trend or lack of it. But with spreads, if you are risk oriented to some extent, a single day of increased volume, especially coming off a series of trendless volume days, is enough to coax one into the market. The closest out-of-the-money OEX call was 235 at 1, a November call and too near expiration. No go. The Dec 235 out-of-the-money (the one to sell) was 3 3/8. The closest in-the-money Dec 230 call (the one to buy) was 5 7/8. Subtracting the 235 call from the 230 call gave us a cost of 2 1/2 or $250 per contract—the right price. So we entered a bull spread. Why not a bear? The closest in-the-money 235 Dec put (to buy) was 6 1/2, the closest out-of-the-money 230 Dec put (to sell) was 4. That too yielded the desired cost of 2 1/2. Why bull over bear? Our market outlook was bullish. Based on what? Nothing in the economic or political news appeared to suggest an end to the bull market, and we had concluded that there would be no old-fashioned general correction but huge single day corrections and some group rotation corrections. It doesn't mean that we wouldn't turn on a dime and switch to a bear spread. We would and did put on both bear and bull spreads simultaneously. Indeed, this seemed like a good time for us to take advantage of highly volatile markets.

With the OEX at 232.20 on November 12, 1986, a bear spread entailed buying the 235 Dec put at 6 1/2 and selling the 230 Dec put at 4 (buying the closest in-the-money option, selling the closest out-of-the-money option). Thus our financial cmotions will be on a teeter-totter. Why can such a thing make sense? We are counting on profitability near-term; we think that volatility will take the market sufficiently up and down before expiration to make both a bull and bear spread profitable.

On November 13 the market dropped 31.50 Dow points. The bear spread licked its chops. The 235 in-the-money put jumped to 10 1/8, the 230 Dec put to 6 5/8. The spread was now 3 1/2. (The bull spread, by contrast, licked its wounds.)

On November 14 the market went up about 11 points; the OEX moved up 1.60. An inconclusive day. Several more followed.

On November 18 the market dropped 43.31 points. The bear spread looked like this: the Dec 235 in-the-money option was at 12 1/8, the 230 at 8 1/8. Thus the spread was at 4, and it would have been wise to take the 1 1/2 points of profit (five contracts times 1 1/2 points equals a profit of $750). To take profit in less than a week is always desirable in spreads, especially in this one where the bull spread was showing a corresponding loss.

Not convinced that we were wrong, we held on for another day. The market moved up about 10 points, taking some of the loss pressure away. (Meanwhile, we also had a combination at work, gainfully employed as it turned out.)

Another day, November 20, brought another reprieve. The condemncd bull spread ate a hearty meal; the index was at 230.33, up 4.61 from the previous day, and the 235 in-the-money call was at 8 1/2, the 230 out-of-the-money call at 4 3/8. So the spread was now at 4 1/8—profitable, since we paid 2 1/2 for it and could now sell it back at a profit of 1 7/8, or about

$938 minus commissions, in just a week. Add that to the $750 and you can see that these spreads can be profitable in a volatile market. Add to that the combination that was working and you have the third profit center. Others would double their profits by doubling the number of contracts from five to ten.

Why didn't we wait for the spread to mature fully and gain the entire 5 points? One should always take 60 percent profit on spreads, in view of the possible ease of such profits and because of the high volatility of markets in which both bull and bear spreads can profit or tail off into losses. As the Dow advances, simultaneous bull and bear spreading may well become the best possible single use of the OEX. Note: you gain 5 points when the spread is full at 5 points. You pay 2 1/2 points.

New Trades

November 21 saw the Dow move up about 33 points, with volume going to 200 million shares from 160 million the day before. The OEX gained 3.65 points, depositing a fiery bull spread on our front door as follows: with the index at 233.68, the 235 out-of-the-money call was now at 2 9/16, the 230 in-the-money at 5 or a bull spread available at 2 7/16. A bargain and we took it. The bear spread that day looked like this: with the OEX at 233.68, the closest in-the-money (the one you buy) put was 235 Dec at 5 3/4; the closest out-of-the-money put (the one you sell) was the Dec 3 3/8. That yielded a cost of 2 3/8 or 1/8 less than the maximum of 2 1/2. We couldn't pass up this bargain.

The market did nothing favorable for our spreads during the next few days. It was a no-lose situation since neither spread was losing (or winning) while our combination was winning.

The market came alive on December 2, jumping 43 Dow points and almost 5 OEX points. That gave our bull spread a profile like this: the Dec 235 out-of-the-money call was at

7 1/8, the Dec 230 in-the-money call at 11 1/2. The bull spread was thus at 3 3/8 versus the 2 1/2 we paid for it. Slim pickings. The bear spread was showing an inevitable loss.

Pearl Harbor day came without incident, since it was on Sunday, and the Japanese were counting their profits not our battleships. The market did nothing December 8, closing up a puny 5 points. One week before expiration, Friday, December 12, the bull spread looked like this: the Dec 235 out-of-the-money call was at 2 7/16; the Dec 230 in-the-money call was at 6, for a spread of 3 9/16, a profit of 1 1/16. The bear spread: the 235 Dec in-the-money was at 2 7/16, the 230 Dec out-of-the-money put at 3/4, or a spread of 1 11/16, versus the 2 7/16 initial cost. So we were losing 5 times 3/4 points, or $375. If we cashed both spreads in on that day we would have been slightly ahead of the game. We waited. Monday was uneventful. Tuesday, three days from expiration, was a day of decision. If the market continued its ho-hum mode we would cash in both spreads, consoled with the profits we had in the combination.

The market moved up on Tuesday, took it back and spurted up at close, settling for a 13 point gain. Nothing decisive occurred throughout the day, taunting our resolve to cast off our two spreads. When irresolution affects the market it casts a similar pallor on market players. The day showed our unresolved results as follows: the index at 238.79 (up almost 2); the bear spread pegged the 235 Dec in-the-money put (no longer in-the-money since the index had risen above the 235 number we had started with) at 7/8, the 230 at 3/16. In other words, no spread. We faced a complete loss here of 2 1/2 points. The bull spread: the 230 at 8 7/8, the 235 at 4, yielding a profit of 4 7/8, or 100 percent of our initial investment of 2 7/16. So the bottom line: $1,250 profit on the bull spread, the same loss on the bear. We lost the commissions. Our belief in the constancy of the bull market was not matched by our faith in the bull spread.

Our pride stung we decided on another bull and bear spread beginning December 19. We expected a Christmas rally of sorts. We also expected more volatility, sufficient to make each spread profitable. Nothing is set in stone, as between theories that support rational expectation and those that merely document personal hopes and fears. Between expectation and hope in these matters there is a wall of gauze that may bind the wounds of failure. Wounds arise because every investor dives into the always uncharted future. Chartists there may be on Wall Street, but they can only get a reading on the past. The best we can ever expect is to deal in probabilities of a rather low incidence of success. That is why we erect hedges.

The OEX index stood at 238.51 on December 19, having risen over 3 points on the day's trading. We liked the fact that volume was steady and higher than the day before and that volume in the industrial average primarily, but also in transportation and utilities, had also picked up. Indeed, it had doubled in utilities. That average, beloved of Dow Jones theorists—who are not fools—should always be checked out before setting sail.

The bull setting: buy the in-the-money OEX option closest to the current index, which was a Jan 235 at 5 1/2 ($550 per contract); sell the out-of-the-money OEX option closest to the index, which was a Jan 240 at 3. The spread was exactly 2 1/2.

The bear setting: the in-the-money OEX put closest to the current index of 238.51 was the 240 Jan, price 6 1/4; the out-of-the-money put closest to the index was 3 1/2. But what have we here? No go. The difference is 2 3/4, which is higher than 2 1/2, so no bear spread could be bought. We thought ruefully that the market didn't know a good thing. Here we were willing to buy it and it wasn't willing to be sold. Should we go ahead with the bull spread and wait a day or two for the tardy bear? Yes.

The market rocked along for a couple of days—no Christmas rally, no Christmas, as the normal stockholder might avow. But we are not normal; we are OEX traders.

For the next few days the volume jumped hysterically, way up, way down. We were both puzzled and frustrated, uncertain both as to direction and strategy. The day after Christmas added no light, since that is a quasi-holiday, with little trading, hence no signals. We forgot the bear spread and took a vacation.

It was the smartest vacation ever. When we returned the market was calm—the calm before the storm, as it turned out. The market had been trading between 1900 and 1940, fitfully, fretfully. It was a perfect trading mode for a combination, the worst possible for any spread. We were tempted to do a bear spread December 30, when the Dow dropped a bit on slightly increased volume—a bearish signal. But we resisted on the theory that spreads need trends and we already owned a bull spread that lacked a trend. One failure is enough. Also, we were bullish. We believed obstinately that the market was going to go up, based on our reading of the tea leaves and my reading of the economic indicators as well as the internals of the market. We sampled opinions on the economy, believing that no bull market ever ended in an ongoing prosperous economy. To be sure, no consensus existed; many economists said flatly the economy wasn't prosperous. We begged to differ.

The one fly in the ointment was that both the utilities and transportation averages had been in an almost steady decline from highs reached around December 1. Dow theorists hold that this kind of divergence does not herald the dawn of a resurgent bull market. But there is always a difference of opinion on whether the divergence was a trend reversal—a transformation of the bull into a bear—or merely a correction. We believed it was a correction. It wasn't an innovation for these divergences to occur; they happen frequently. So we waited for a clearer signal before taking another plunge. Remember our overall position; we held a combination that was working perfectly and would result in a 100 percent gain. We also held a bull spread that wasn't working at all and threatened us with if not a 100 percent loss, certainly some kind of a loss. So we were wary. One must always assess one's total position in light of the economy and see how one relates if at all. That entails considerations of the sort listed above.

On New Year's Eve, having nothing better to do, we checked out our bull spread. The Jan 235, for which we paid 5 1/2, was now at 1 13/16; the Jan 240, which had cost 3, was now 3/4. We were losing much of our entire spread at this point (five contracts) and wondered whether to get drunk or sober. The spread had narrowed from 2 1/2 to 1 1/16, meaning that instead of gaining (by widening from 2 1/2 to 5, potentially) it had narrowed to 1 1/16. We paid $1,250, hoping that it would double. It was now worth under $600 and fading fast. But expiration was not until the third Friday of January, so we held out. The New Year's Eve gloom did accomplish one thing; it disabled us from putting on a bear spread. We decided that while we knew where the market was going (onward and upward) it just couldn't make up its own mind.

January 2 was the day the market made up its mind. On low volume the Dow spurted up 31 points, the OEX moved up 4, placing our bull spread in a much friendlier role. The Jan 235 call was now 3 1/2; the Jan 240 was 1 3/8. The spread was looking up; it was now 2 1/8.

Monday, January 5, 1987, saw the Dow move up 44 points, flaring up in the last hour of trading. The OEX gained 5.44 points. The bull spread now looked like this: the Jan 235 call was 6 7/8; the Jan 240 was 3 3/8, for a spread of 3 1/2, for a profit of 1 or $500 (five contracts). On January 7 the Dow moved up another 19 points, OEX jumped 2. The spread was now at 4 and we cashed it in, taking $800 profit (minus commission).

Had we waited two more days our profit would have been close to $1,700 or almost the total possible gain. But pigs too often go to slaughter, as we have to keep reminding ourself.

To Market, to Market

The industrials, transportations and utilities were now moving up in tandem, reassuring our judgment that their earlier divergence was merely a correction. Volume was increasing almost day by day, suggesting that more and more institutions were coming to market. Another bull spread looked ripe. But so did the buying of calls and an S&P 500 stock index futures contract. We splurged on all three.

The OEX index was at 244 on January 8. The bull spread was too expensive at 3 3/16. A bear spread had the right price but we did not want to go against the market trend, which was now emphatically bullish.

The OEX closed at 245.45 on January 9. The closest in-the-money OEX call to the index was a Feb 245 priced at 5; the closest out-of-the-money OEX call to the index was a Feb 250, priced at 2 3/4. Subtracting the two numbers yields 2 1/4, which is below 2 1/2 and thus a bargain basement price for a bull spread. We bought five contracts at $1,125.

On January 14, with the Dow up 22 points, the OEX gained 3 points. The Feb 245 call was at 6 3/4; the Feb 250 moved to 3 7/8, to widen the spread to 2 7/8.

Another day, another dollar on January 15. The OEX closed up 3.47 in response to a huge volume that sent the Dow up almost 36 points. Pretty poor response, since the OEX is supposed to move 1 point for every 7 Dow points and it did not. That's one of the most predictable frustrations in OEX trading. One learns to live with it or leave it. We had to live with it and take profit, slim as it might be, since expiration was breathing down our neck on January 16. During the next trading day, January 16—expiration day—the Dow moved up sharply in the morning and we were able to cash in the spread for a gain of a single point of $500. It had been a rash move that didn't actually fail without living up to our heady expectations.

We decided to go back in, since we did make $500 on a week's work in the OEX pits.

Around noon on January 16 we put on another bull spread. We sold the Mar 255 call at 5 1/2 and bought the Mar 250 call at 8, thus gaining a 2 1/2 point spread. Why so far out? Nothing in February met the 2 1/2 point spread requirement and we were anxious to be in the market in view of its explosive upward bias.

Monday, January 19, saw the OEX close up 4 points. The Mar 255 call, bought at 5 1/2, made a huge jump to 10 1/4, the Mar 250 call, bought at 8, jumped to 12 1/2.

January 20 and 21 were uneventful. January 22 the market leaped up 51.60, with the Mar 255 call at 13 3/4, the 250 call at 16. Progress.

January 23 was the record smashing day up and down, ending 44 points down. The OEX dropped 4.47 points. This was shocking for combination sellers, call buyers and the S&P 500 index futures, all of which we owned. The bull spread showed the 255 call at 11 1/2, the 250 call at 13 3/4. Not much movement. More than 300 million shares changed hands that Friday on a wild roller coaster ride. The Dow moved from 2200 to 2065 (approximately) on an intraday move of more than 135 points. The OEX had a 13 point ride, but ending only 4.47 points down.

On Monday the Dow debacle tried to clear itself away, first dropping somewhat then righting itself and moving up, closing off its high for the day with a small 5.76 point gain. The OEX hardly moved, though it shuffled around during the day. The Mar 255 call was at 11 3/4; the 250 was at 15. No cigar.

The gods smiled on January 28, widening the spread. The Mar 255 call was now 13 1/2, the 250 call was 18, a 4 1/2 point spread. We took it, netting $2,250, minus commissions, for a period of twelve days.

This spread showed that you can go out in time without sacrificing the touchstone of the spread tactic—the opportunity for quick profit. This was the opposite tactic of the previous spread that we took on with expiration day looming in about two weeks. For that one we paid the price of our hubris; we got by with only the skin of our teeth intact. But note the results: $500 for that one and we had to hold it through the teeth-chattering expiration date (the morning), whereas the new one, over about the same period of time, brought in almost the total amount possible. The leisurely approach was its own reward. We decided to make a late New Year's resolution: think ahead for the date of the spread.

While this spread was in force, and obviously working well, we decided to try another tactic, an overlapping spread, commencing January 26, with the OEX at 259.28, using a February expiration. We wanted to see how it would compare with the March expiration date of the spread already in force.

The Feb 260, closest in-the-money, was 6 1/4; the closest out-of-the-money was the Feb 265 at 4 1/8. In other words, another bargain basement sale for 2 1/8 or $212.00. Five contracts made the cost about $1,060, the maximum loss possible. Ten contracts, a more common speculation, doubles it, also doubling the potential profit.

A week later the OEX was around 265, the spread at 3. Market action had been generally favorable, with some backing and filling. On Thursday, February 5, our first soul-searching decision arrived. Though the Dow closed down 14.62, the OEX went up 2 points. This paradox cannot be explained without digging through every stock in the S&P 100, but it provided a spread of 4 and posed the Hamlet option question; to cash in or not to cash in the spread.

We decided to do nothing, since expiration was ten trading

days away and the market seemed to be continuing its strong advance. The next few days produced only anxiety; the market backed off and the spread narrowed from 4 to 3 1/2. The Friday before expiration, February 13, saw a Dow gain of 17 points and an OEX move up of almost 4. That brought the Feb 260 call to 9 7/8, the Feb 265 to 5 5/8—a spread of 4 1/4. What to do? Expiration was only five trading days off, and our rule was to take 60 percent profits. We had passed that mark. We followed the rule, receiving $2,125 for the spread. It had cost $1,060, giving us a profit of $1,065, in less than three weeks.

Ring in the New

Having wrung out the old spreads at a tidy profit, it was time to ring in the new. Market volatility, throughout the big surge that had taken place in the previous six weeks, had increased. Volume shot up, then down, and intraday swings were wider and scarier, all due to program trading. Since Friday, February 13, was our lucky day, we thought it well to plunge in again. With the OEX at 268.67, with volume veering towards the 200 million level, and with continuing wide intraday swings, we were leery but intoxicated with success. This mood, once invoked by Stalin to quell a burst of optimism among the comrades who thought they had passed the capitalists in the production of pigs, should be suppressed by every investor. It leads usually to the kind of ruination practiced by comrade Stalin. But forewarned is forearmed only in spy circles. We rushed to put on a new spread. Lo, the ghost of Stalin, as no bull spread was available to us on that lucky Friday. The right strike prices offered a spread of 3 instead of the requisite 2 1/2.

What about a bear spread? Again, we shied away, the memory of our failure earlier when we ran both a bull and bear spread, the bull winning the bear losing.

The spread remained at 3 the next day. It continued to elude our grasp, as the market sputtered for a few days until

February 20. The OEX closed at 275.06 with the Mar 275 closest in-the-money at 5 7/8, the Mar 280 closest out-of-the-money at 3 7/8 for another big bargain at 2. In a bull market episode of this sort, with the market sitting on a long upward sweep from 1900 to a perch of 2235 (but brief in time, since it had started January 2), one could be pardoned for being suspicious of a new bull spread. But if you've had the success of a half dozen or more profitable trades under your belt, conventional fears of market correction would cut very little ice, especially as the cost of the new spread—2 points—was so low.

The five contracts, at a mere $1,000, looked irresistible, even though there were only twenty trading days before expiration.

A week later, February 27, the spread was narrower than the 2 points we paid. But on March 4, a 31 point Dow advance pushed the OEX up almost 5 points and widened the spread to 3. We were now in the black by $500. By March 12 the spread was at 3 1/2. But expiration was only about a week away. This kind of dilemma is the OEX player's cross. It's a form of Russian roulette, which the ordinary investor may not wish to play. A 3 1/2 spread meant a profit of 1 1/2 times 5 contracts or $750 profit. This was since February 20.

More conservative players would have taken the profit; Russian roulette players would not. Let's join the Russians for the nonce. Note that anyone in this spread would have been in a pretty good spot, since it would have taken a very sharp decline in the OEX (and the Dow) to push the spread into the red. But better spread than red, so our advice was to charge ahead. Remember that these trades were ongoing, recommended in the *Hume MoneyLetter*, recommended also to Hume subscribers who called me by phone, some undertaken by me from time to time.

Another Friday the 13 (March) was an unlucky day; the spread narrowed again, cutting into profits. We entered the last week with somewhat flickering hopes and some burgeoning angst—the worst kind. The spread, on Monday, was 2 5/8, the profits declining. But Tuesday brought cheer. The OEX leaped almost 5 points, widening the spread to 3 once again. We held on and were both rewarded and frazzled. The market leaped 34 points, the OEX jumped 4 1/2 and the spread by noon was around 4 1/2. We took the 2 1/2 profit or $250 per contract. Since we had paid only 2 ($200 per contract) our profit was five times $250. Thus we waited to the bitter end, only this time the end was our friend.

What Next?

On Monday, March 23, the market continued its romp into high ether, moving up 30 points, sending the OEX up 3 1/2 to 291.73. Could this ecstatic spiral continue on and on, like melodies in a Rachmaninov concerto? The Stalin syndrome, "flushed with success," reasserted itself. You recall that Stalin's method of correcting anything was to murder, to jail or to suppress (or all three at once). But how to apply that to the now flighty market? Should we kill the goose that had been laying all those golden eggs? The OEX? Jail it? Suppress it? Banish it? Only a congressman or Stalinist would make such a suggestion.

We decided, instead, to suppress our latent Stalinism. We bought another bull spread.

Quit Stalin

A May spread beckoned. With the OEX at 292.06, we entered a May 290 to 295 spread. May 290, the closest in-the-money leg cost 10 1/2; May 295, the closest out-of-the-money leg listed at 8, thus giving us the requisite 2 1/2 spread. The date was May 24, so we had ample time to win or lose, and we anticipated not having to go through the tightening noose that we fashioned for ourselves in April, when we had to wait until the last possible minute to catch the golden goose. This, we hoped, would be a more leisurely flight.

The next few days didn't turn out that way. The market retracted somewhat, dropping a few points here and there, and while not exactly hair-tearing, this was not soothing. Our cause became hopeless on March 30 when the spread narrowed to around 1 1/2. But it was a typical blue Monday and we resolved to give the week another chance, since there was so much time remaining until the third Friday in May. The next day set matters aright, with an OEX gain of almost 7 points and a Dow gain of almost 70! The spread: the 290 at 9 3/4, the 295 at 7 1/2, for a total of 2 1/4. Nothing to write home about, but nothing to worry your mother about, either.

For the next week the market declined or marked time. So did the OEX.

By Tuesday, April 14, the market was plunging down, taking our hopes for the bull spread with it. A bear spread was beginning to look wise, but possibly too late. The spread was down to 1 point and we were losing about $750. But we had a whole month until expiration. Intense market volatility began to rocket the market up and down in big swings, making us regret our failure to have a bear as well as bull spread. Regrets earn very little money.

By the end of April the market correction—for that is what it was—had about run its course, leaving the bull spread at a wan 1, which meant about $500 in the red. But April showers bring May flowers, to put a nontechnical analysis on the hopes we continued to possess. May Day produced the usual rocket launchers in Red Square but no rockets in the market; it declined a bit, shooting down our bull spread one more time.

Optimism returned May 5, when the Dow gained 52 points, the OEX almost 7 and our spread removed its death pallor; it was 2 1/4 or almost at break even. The index stood at 291.26.

A bullish bias continued on as the Dow soared briefly from 2338 up to 2369 during the day's trading Wednesday, May 6. Had we been nimble enough, we could have cashed in the spread. It moved above 4, briefly. We weren't and didn't. On the finale, the market finished up only about 4 points, leaving the spread at 2 1/4.

Bad news was the order of the next three trading days, and we were getting close to expiration (or execution) day, May 15. We took our lumps Thursday, when the market opened down and continued that way, even though it was up over 10 points during the day. We got out on a spread of 1 point, with a loss of $750 instead of a profit of 4 1/8, which was there May 6. That, as the French say, is life, and, as we say, hard times but not enough of it.

Much Later

The spreads above are as useful as the more recent examples to follow from 1989 and 1990. The market offered opportunities then as now. Then the market was clearly in a bullish and continuing expansion, not without its corrections. Now, as I write in 1990, the market is in an undecided phase. Many analysts declare that we are in a bear market, others say the bull is alive but not kicking. That would take a much brighter economic picture. The OEX picture, by contrast, is bright and shining.

Because of the potential for devastating losses in naked positions, such as in selling combinations of OEX 100 options, and the huge margin costs now exacted, we see such activity as a too-risky ploy for all but the most seasoned traders.

Bull and bear spreads, by contrast, offer opportunity for hedging, if you have market direction right. It's always a big if, unlike our vertical spreads in Strategy One where you are hedged in any market. So, after these several years have passed since the crash, it is vital that in order to make OEX trading once again no riskier than any other, we posit a new pecking order of trades.

Our "out-of-the-money vertical selling" or spreading is our first strategy. We have already shown that the amount of risk is acceptable in all markets, which was the first condition we sought in a strategy, given the volatility of modern markets. The amount of profit potential, while less than in combination or "strangle" selling, can surpass 15 percent, and if you do it often enough can generate big profits. How much profit depends on the individual, the amount of margin (number of contracts) and the broker.

OEX trading, as we've noted, is exciting and risky. The vertical spread of Strategy One eliminates much of the risk as it diminishes part of the excitement. Depending on your own need for excitement in financial dealings, you may prefer the more dangerous strategies that follow Strategy One.

Depending on the market, a complete hedge can be a big bore or a big blast. You can buy a put and a call (five, ten or more) and be completely hedged. If the market suddenly lurches up or down, you will make a lot of money given the right choice of strike price, even though the losing side may turn out to be a total loss. On rare occasions you can strike it rich on both sides, if you buy enough time and the market cooperates. Such a journey can be as exciting as the most dangerous naked option position but without the risks. It should be said that the odds against winning both sides of such a spread are as prohibitively high as betting on the Chicago Cubs to enter the World Series.

Let's look at spread results beginning in December 1989, several years after our last lunge at them.

On December 13, 1989, we inclined toward a bull spread to take advantage of the customary Christmas rally that was going on. It was very reckless; expiration was only two days away but we had been doing pretty well lately. The OEX was at 331. Nearest in-the-money call (the one you buy), the 330, was 2 3/4. Nearest out-of-the-money call (the one you sell), the 335, was 1/2. It qualified since it cost less than 2 1/2. We bought five calls for 2 3/4 ($1,375) and sold five calls for 1/2 ($250).

On December 14, the market rose 10 points by noon; the OEX was up less than 2. The rest of the day was inconclusive. Expiration day, December 15, was just that for our spread. The market dropped from the opening bell and then seesawed until closing. We withdrew on one of the seesaws, with a 2 1/2 point loss.

The chief point of this trade was that it was too reckless; too close to expiration. We wanted to go out to the next month but could find no bull spread there, and because the market had been moving up sharply we thought it was a risk worth doing. It wasn't. Plenty of good trades happen in one or two days but when you throw in a nearby expiration date you are compounding the odds against you, unbearably. You have no time in which to correct mistakes.

On Tuesday, December 19, 1989, we were again on the prowl for a bull spread with the OEX at 321. But the only spreads we could find that qualified were bear spreads. We usually believe that the market knows more about its plans than we do, and when the market growled "this is no bull; do a bear spread," we obliged.

We bought the Jan 325s for 7 and sold the Jan 320s for 5—good deal, less than $2.50 spread.

For the next few days the OEX went up slowly, past 325 to 327. The bear spread appeared to be hibernating. Then a real jolt, on January 2 the Dow zoomed up and the OEX went up almost 7 points. The spread was almost worthless. But matters began to show some promise and on January 5 the OEX took a tumble back to 329.55. That did no more than lift hopes briefly, only to be dashed the next day. By January 10, with only seven more trading days, the spread was exactly where we put it on—2 points apart. That meant we at least had no loss other than the commission. But the Dow had a major drop of 70 points, Friday, January 12, and the bear peeked its head above water. Expiration was only four days away, and huge drops often are followed by sideways motion. Should we get out while the getting was good? The decision: tough it out.

The papers were full of gloomy forecasts about the U.S. economy, the Japanese market, Gorbachev's troubles in Baku; suddenly Russia had moved into the financial markets after a seventy-two year hiatus.

The bear spread widened the next day to 3, which means a 1 point profit. We held on, stubbornly. The market dropped 33 points on Wednesday and the spread widened to 4 points. We decided to wait for the morning bell Thursday. The market started out indecisively and we emerged with a near 2-point victory, looking like this: the 325s (bought for 7) finished at 5; giving us 2 points of loss. The 320s, sold for 5, finished at 1 1/4, giving us 3 3/4 points of profit, or a total of 1 3/4 profit. That's about $875. Not much for the time period but worth doing. Ten contracts would have doubled the amount; twenty contracts would quadruple it, etc. Three years ago these spreads required no margin, but the crash ended that free lunch. Would twenty contracts require $20,000 in margin? It varies; ask your broker.

Late in January the market had been dropping systematically, including the 77-point drop January 22. This had taken the market from all-time high territory over 2840 back down to below 2600, a correction of over 10 percent. Despite the continuing gloomy economic news, and the growls of the bears now in a gathering crescendo, it seemed that the market was ready to do a quick reform, a bounce at least. Top and bottom fishing are the oldest sports in market timing. Unfortunately, the biggest ones usually get away; the biggest top fish of all,

October 19, 1987, went unnoticed by most market timers, with notable exceptions. Nevertheless, a 10 percent move is often a signal to big players that enough is enough already; it is time to put on a new record, a new song. We went looking for a bull spread now with our Sherlock Holmes magnifying glass.

We waited to see whether the dust would settle. The market continued to decline, slowly now, with some thrashing around, like the wounded beast it was. But perhaps it was ready for reform, like other old scoundrels. Paddy Bauler, an old Chicago ward heeler, used to say, "Chicago ain't ready for reform," a verdict richly confirmed then and forever more. The market is a lot like that; it can go on a drunken spree, then do a Sunday school turnabout to seduce the most prim moralizer.

Now we looked for a bull spread, having lost out on our last effort. We found none; we returned to the bear camp. With February expiration almost four weeks away, we lit on another bargain basement spread. We bought five Feb 310 puts for 6 1/2; we sold five Feb 305 puts for 4 5/8. The OEX was at 310. The five Feb 305 puts we sold for 4 5/8 brought in $2,312. Thus the bear spread cost $938 plus commissions on January 24.

On the next day the market took another dive, the Dow dropping 43 points, widening our bear spread to a welcome 2 1/2 points. (We welcome every gain.)

Friday, January 26, saw the OEX trade in a range of 308 and 300, with a close at 305. When it hit 300 in the morning our spread touched 4 points, and while we were staring at the screen wondering whether or not to let the money fall into our lap, the market changed course and went up, narrowing the spread.

On Monday, January 29, the Dow went down again, but not enough. While the OEX was as low as 301, our spread never moved much above 3.

Tuesday saw another dropping market and this time we were able to reach a decision of near 4 points. The spread was only about a week old, so any profit was worth taking. He who hesitates is poor.

It wound up like this: we paid 1 7/8 for the spread; when we cashed it in we received 3 7/8, so we wound up with 2 points profit times 5. That's $1,000 minus commissions for a week's work in the pits (our living room chair).

Was it now time for the elusive bull spread? We sought out the oracle, Mother NYSE. On Friday, February 2, we met our bull. Putting this as delicately as possible, he/she/it went like this: the OEX was at 309; we sold the Feb 310 calls (five of them) for 4, we bought five of the 315 calls for 1 7/8. This yields a spread of 2 1/8, a trifle higher than we've been paying for the bear spreads, but that's the nature of the beast. In a market like this, the bulls tend to run a little richer, as in Pamplona.

The most important fact about this trade is that it bends the rule, announced elsewhere in this chapter, that you buy the in-the-money OEX option nearest the OEX strike price, and you sell the out-of-the-money OEX option nearest the OEX strike price. If we had followed this rule precisely with the OEX at 309, we would have bought the 305s for 7 1/8 and sold the 310s for 4, thus buying a spread of 3 1/8, which would have been the road to ruin. But the rule above, like many another, admits of minor exceptions.

One reason we were anxious to use a bull spread rather than another bear, in addition to the reasons above, is that we were not the only optioneers looking for a market move upwards. Well over 100,000 more bulls than bears were of this mindset. If these numbers translate into buyers of stocks and options, the market will go up. Nothing having to do with markets translates into so simple a formula, but optioneers grasp at straws if straws are the only clues we have. There were others, as noted; the market was due for a move up after the weeks of selling. In other words, that dandy, Mr. Oversold, has waltzed into view.

On the following day the market did nothing. The OEX closed up about 1 point, with the spread widening ever so slightly, 1/8.

Tuesday's results were worse; the OEX dropped 2 points. The Feb 310s, bought for 4, were now 2 15/16, the Feb 315s, sold for 1 7/8, were now 1 3/16.

The next day was much better; the Dow swooped up 34 points after dropping 20. Too bad it couldn't have gained 54 starting from ground zero. Nevertheless, the OEX responded well by moving up 5 points. Now our bull spread was glowing and growing. The Feb 310s, sold for 4, were 6, the 315s, bought for 1 7/8, were 3. The spread itself was 3; we were well in the black if Mother NYSE continued to smile.

She failed on Thursday, moving fitfully, and dropping the OEX a trifle or less than a point.

Friday went nowhere; the OEX closed up .35.

Matters went from bad to worse. For the next three days the market moved sideways, as did our spread. However, on Thursday the outlook brightened. The OEX went up 4 points and our spread looked like this: the Feb 310s were 5 3/8; the Feb 315s were 1 5/16. We cashed it. In this world you learn to sweat out expiration days without shuffling off this mortal coil yourself.

Our winnings were 4 1/16 on a spread that was 2 1/8 when we entered it. So our net gain was 1 15/16 or almost 2. Not bad for nine trading days. In dollars: $193.75 × 5 equals $968.75.

The moral of this spread is that bull and bear spreads can be nerve-wracking but you can win at them by paying as little as possible. In this case we paid less than 2, while violating the spread rule, as noted earlier—buy the in-the-money strike price nearest the OEX level, sell the nearest out-of-the-money strike price nearest the OEX level. We should have bought the 305s and sold the 310s, but we bought the 310s and sold the 315s because the 305–310 combination was far too expensive.

Another trade we did in January, actually earlier but more or less coextensive with it—and overlapping these trades is often an excellent procedure—took place on Thursday, January 18. We had done a good vertical spread, described elsewhere. We also bought three Feb 310 puts for $500 each and one Feb 325 call for $300. We wanted a hedge. We were nervous about the market. We also put on a bear spread in anticipation of a plunge. Why did I believe the market was about to jump off the cliff? The Japanese stock market was frayed around the edges. It had taken a deep plunge and though it seemed to stabilize, the Japanese market was in uncharted waters. Interest rates there were at dangerously high levels, higher than at any recent time. There was near civil war in the U.S.S.R., with perestroika and Gorbachev in a Russian stew, posing difficult consequences for the economies of the West. A resumption of Stalinism, for example, could again disrupt Western economies. Japan was concerned and involved; there had been an economic and political opening to the U.S.S.R., with the possibility of great projects and political settlements.

So too in Europe, where U.S. interests were at stake. Market technicians may scoff at such fundamentalist doctrine, but such events can control market direction, especially on a short term. Closer to home there was much disappointment over corporate profitability with too many dismal fourth quarter results coming in each day. Also, the Federal Reserve was sticking to its anti-inflationary pose, against the urging of the Bush Administration. The Fed was cornered by the rising tide of interest rates in both Europe and Japan, especially in West Germany, where rates were above ours. Who would buy our Treasury paper if our rates were no higher than those of Germany and Japan?

The market had made new all-time highs above 2800, where it faltered, unsurprisingly. It was heavily overbought at that point. Many argued that in light of lowered corporate profitability, the market was also over valued. A correction of some heft was in order. It might take weeks and months to sort itself out. Overhanging everything was the Hamlet-like question of recession, was it to be or not to be?

These were the basic reasons for my own view of a market drop. I did not, however, believe we faced immediate recession or a major bear market, as many were predicting.

Technicians of the market would say this kind of fundamental analysis won't work in volatile markets using the OEX. Nobody knows for sure what indicators work at any precise moment. You must try to think of everything that might affect the market at that moment in time. Technical considerations such as volume, the advance/decline ratio, etc., are always with market action. We must get behind them to find and assess other factors that might be coming into play at just that moment.

The bear spread we addressed went like this. The OEX was at 317. We bought the 320 Mar put at 10 3/4 and sold the 315 Mar put at 9, with five contracts each. So the cost was 1 3/4.

Observe that the type of spreads we have thus far pursued won't enable you to cope with huge market drops or gains, those one-day calamities or gains that increasingly characterize our markets. For that you need buy puts and calls in sufficient amount and as far out in time as you can afford.

On Friday, January 19, 1990, which was expiration day for the Jan options, the market dropped frighteningly in the morning, recovered and finished slightly ahead with the OEX completing the day where it began the day before, at 317. Though we were tempted to take a 3 point gain on our puts, we resisted, luckily for us as it turned out.

Monday, January 22, was another red letter day. The market nose-dived 77 points in a rash of fearful reports about earnings and higher interest rates in the teeth of rising Japanese and German rates. The OEX fell almost 9 1/2 points, to close at 310. (Had we bought in-the-money puts we would have cleaned up.)

The Feb 310 puts were at 8, giving us a profit of 2 1/2 points. The call had a loss of 1 1/8, so we were still ahead. The bear spread: Mar 320 put bought at 10 3/4 was now at 15 3/4, the Mar 315 put we had sold was at 13 1/2. So the spread had widened from the opening margin of 1 3/4 to 2 1/4.

The next day was no cigar. The market went up slightly, so did the OEX. It closed at 312. The Feb 325 call dropped a little more. The spread dropped a little of its gain. Another day another yawn.

January 22, day three of these proceedings, was a mini-quake. The market took another big hit. It dropped 60 points (Dow) in the morning; the bear spread came close at one point to spreading out 5 points. The OEX was down 6 points. We took what we could get, towards the close of the trading. The market dropped 77 points; OEX dropped 9 1/2 points to 310.

We sold the Feb 310 puts for a gain of 2 1/2 or $750 (3 puts × $250). We were holding one Feb 325 call that cost $300 and had lost about half its value. Our spread profits were 4 1/8 or $2,063 minus the cost of the spread initially, which was 1 3/4 or $875. The total take therefore came to $1,188. These proceedings were compressed into a four-day (trading days) period, January 18 to 22. If you add the $875 spread profit to the $750 gain from the Feb 310 puts we bought, the total is $1,625. But you have to figure that the Feb 325 call, now off by half, could turn out to be a total loss, but only $300.

On January 24, 1990, two days after the big market drop, we commenced another five-contract bear spread with the OEX at 310. Nearest in-the-money put was the Feb 310 for 6 1/2; nearest out-of-the-money put was the Feb 305 at 4 5/8. So the cost was another bargain at 1 7/8. In dollars that is 5 × $187 or $935.

The market took a 43.46 point dive the next day in a late afternoon splurge of program selling. No special news event was fingered. If you rounded up the usual suspects, they would include government statistics on growth, a negative number tossed around by gloomy analysts who sell gloom by the bushel. Traffic in gloom always outsells its opposite number. Also, there were rumblings from Japan that perhaps the U.S. Treasury paper market might no longer be their cup of sake. The new Japanese co-prosperity sphere (World War II euphemism for the Berlin-Tokyo axis) might not include their most intimate former trading partner, at least for the time being. It was enough to rustle a few Wall Street kimonos. Our kimono (spread) now looked like this: the OEX was at 306; the 310s, bought at 6 1/2, were now 9 1/2; the 305s, sold at 4 5/8, were 7. So the spread had only widened from 1 7/8 to 2 1/2.

I noted the Feb 310 puts we sold for 8 on January 22 were now at 9 1/2. Why so frivolous a deed in a falling market? We were caught up in the excitement of the spread working so quickly and thought it best to take every profit in sight. Ecstasy and panic are not the best guides to rational behavior, if there is such a thing.

On January 26, the Dow was again on a slippery slope. At 3 p.m. or thereabouts it was down about 30 points. Our spread was a rosy-cheeked 4 points. We decided to take it on the possibility that the pervasive gloom might trigger an upward reaction.

It was easy enough to take; we made off with $2,000 minus the cost of $935, or $1,065 minus commissions.

On Tuesday, January 30, 1990, the OEX was around 300. When it was 303 a bear spread was available for 2 ($200 for each of five contracts). We bought the Feb 305 puts for 7 3/8, we sold the Feb 300 puts for 5 3/8.

Though volume on the NYSE had been trending up in late January, causing some unease about market direction, we continued to believe in bear spreads, especially as no bull spreads qualified. As I have stressed, it is not wise to fool with Mother NYSE; if she says the bears are ruling the roost, as in this case in which no bull spread cost 2 1/2 or less, one goes with the bears.

On Wednesday the Dow moved up 47 points; the bulls rambled up from the opening bell. Our bear spread was an inevitable casualty on its opening skirmish. The spread narrowed.

The market moved mostly sideways on February 2, finishing up slightly. Our bear slumbered.

The next trading day was not better. The market rallied, the OEX finished at 309, up almost 2 points. Our bear was weakening.

We decided to put on a bull spread, if that was the way the cookie was disintegrating. We did note, however, that the market finished far below its highs of the day. Whistling in the dark is one of the hit parade songs of the options players.

Unfortunately there were no bull spreads; spread players, like stock buyers and market analysts, can also miss the bull.

So we bought three calls—three April 325s for 5 or $1500, to go with our earlier call bought back on January 18, the Feb 325, that had lost some of its deathly pallor (it was now an anemic 3/8, up from 1/16).

On the next trading day, February 5, the April 325 calls, bought for 5 points, remained at 5, the Feb 325 single call, bought at 3, was now at 5/16. Our call buying would win few awards at this point. The bear spread would win nothing. It was at 1 1/8.

February 6 saw the OEX trade between 310 and 306.5, and finish at 308 for a loss of almost 2 points. The Dow fell 12 points over worries that the U.S. Treasury refunding would not attract enough Japanese and German buying, according to the *Wall Street Journal,* which talks to people who say such things. The Dow opened at 2618, dropped as low as 2588, and closed at 2606. The spread actually widened at one point to a tempting 3 points which would have chickened us out more or less even. Much as we love chicken we had bigger game in mind. The spread, however, finished the day at 1 point! Fowl!

Trading on February 7 sent the bear spread into an almost catatonic state. The OEX traded between 313 and 305, closing at 313 for a gain of 5. The calls revived. The Apr 325s, for which we paid 5, were now at 6 1/4. The Feb 325 was at 1/2. What to do? Pray.

February 8 saw the Dow jump sharply from 2640 to 2663 around 11 a.m. At that point we were in a semi-trauma of indecision. Our calls were okay—the profitable 325s were up to 7 1/4, meaning that we had 2 1/4 points of profit or $675. We took it. And the spread? The spread was dead. It was time to compose a requiem for the spread. (It was under 1 point.)

Friday, a week away from expiration, went like this. The Dow meandered up and down. Opening at 2645, it eventually closed at 2648. It looked like an uneasy weekend.

On Monday, February 12, the OEX lost about 3 points. The Dow dropped 29 points in fairly slow trading, led down by the imminent collapse of Drexel Burnham Lambert. Noted for its junk bond meteoric rise, its equally rapid demise under the hammer of the New York prosecutor, whose zeal in bringing it to bay on charges of racketeering appalled much of the U.S. financial industry, Drexel Burnham looked like a symbol of a market uncertain of its future.

We were looking for help on Tuesday; we didn't get it. The OEX traded narrowly, closing at 311, leaving the spread at 1/2 with three days until expiration. We had a small loss in the Feb 325 call and a larger loss in the spread. We knew the call was worthless (it was 1/16) and we believed that the market had not fully discounted the Drexel Burnham disaster. Hence we expected a fall. It was a wallflower situation; we sat patiently, awaiting a connection between our hopes and reality, knowing that the clock was ticking and the dance would soon be over.

What should we have done? It was too late. We had a chance to leave a losing trade with no loss. We didn't take it. So we decided to tough it out to expiration and a potential loss of about $1,000. One day's drop of 50 or more points would have erased that loss, with three days remaining. Larry Spears, a financial journalist, has written that one should accept such losses gracefully. Thus one might achieve grace through loss, along with the pain of red ink.

The spread consisted of Feb 305 puts bought for 7 3/8, and the Feb 300 puts sold for 5 3/8. At February 13 the 305s were 1, the 300s were 1/2. The spread was deflated.

Elsewhere matters were different. The vertical spreads were doing well, along with the calls we had bought and sold profitably. We faced the loss of the single Feb 325 call, at $300. Thus, while we weren't exactly affluent as a consequence of OEX trading, we were profitable.

On Thursday the Dow went up, and with it our hopes went up (in smoke) insofar as the January 30 spread was concerned. We lost about $950 on it, plus $300 on the Feb 325 call.

Alternate Strategy

One way to avoid or mitigate loss is through what I call alternate strategy. To that end we will examine trades from the end of January 1990 to expiration in February, to compare with trades over the same period illustrated herein. The purpose of this exercise is to see whether similar trades, slightly different in time and price may have similar outcomes. We're looking at the same trade—bear and bull spreading—with different entry points.

We already had one bear spread; an advantageous bull spread was not available so we were reduced to a competitor bear.

The date was January 18, 1990, the OEX was at 317. We bought the 320 Mar put at 10 3/4 and sold the 315 Mar put at 9, with five contracts each. The cost was 1 3/4, or bargain basement.

Remember that a grand OEX strategy requires more than one market entry; you cannot just have a bear or bull spread, or the much more dangerous "strangle" out there by itself. These combinations are all at the mercy of market volatility, day to day, which is not predictable by man or beast, woman or god (there is dispute about the latter since Elaine Garzarelli's track record was posted and god is yet to be heard from).

To cope with market crisis—unexpected giant moves up or down but mostly down—you must buy both puts and calls in sufficient amount and as far out as you can afford, to cover all your other market activities. I will not say that it is the only way to win, but it is the only way to avoid catastrophic losses. Vince Lombardi is supposed to have said that winning is the only thing. I say not losing everything is the only thing. It should be noted that our vertical spread strategy assures that you cannot lose everything. Indeed, it almost comes to the point that you cannot lose anything, if you are alert, determined, conscientious, aggressive, creative, assured of your place in the universe, with a toothpaste smile and an hourglass figure, with a broker to match.

Analysts have many reasons for their behavior and that of the market—two different entities that rarely coincide. In the old days explanations were based on the fact that the market was controlled by the public. Today markets are controlled by huge fund managers and professional traders—super sophisticates. To make matters worse—more difficult—markets are now international. Hence to predict market movement is to predict the thinking of the super sophisticates who control the markets. Are they bulls? Bears? Technicians? Fundamentalists? To ask these relevant questions is to show that there are no relevant answers. Thus the individual investor must be defensive at all times.

So why not do vertical spreads twenty-four hours daily, twice as often as we indicate in our trading schedule under Strategy One, if they are so riskless? You could do much worse, but vertical spreads work best only in a sideways market, whereas bull and bear spreads flourish in moving markets. Vertical spreads in a moving market either cause small losses or postpone profits and cast a pall over the idea of trading; they can enrich your broker but gain you nothing. Thus the idea of an alternate strategy must always intrude, especially when you are winning. That is the time when, if you repeat what you are doing, you will almost certainly lose.

At the point in time we refer to, January 18, 1990, we were running two bear spreads, undertaken about a week apart. On the new one, we watched the first day go against it.

The next trading day, January 22, 1990, is famous for its 77 Dow point loss. The OEX dropped almost 9 1/2 points. The new spread looked like this: the 320 Mar put (the one we bought) was at 15 3/4, up from 10 3/4. The 315 Mar put (the one we sold at 9) was now at 13 1/2. It was disappointing that so huge a drop did not produce a wider spread. There have been 45 point moves in the Dow that produced a 5 point spread. The malevolent options god strikes again.

The next day was inconclusive, the OEX ending about where it began. So too on Wednesday, January 24. The spread: 3 points with the 320s at 14 1/2, the 315s at 11 1/2.

On Thursday, January 25, the Dow fell 43 1/2 points, the OEX closed down 4. The Mar 320s were 18 3/8, the 315s were at 14 7/8. Why not more movement? Because we had gone out to March, an extra month, in effect. We did cash in the other bear spread we were holding, but kept this one in the hope that we would gain the entire 5 points (we had a profit of 4 1/8 on the other one), mostly to see how practical it was to hold two bear spreads undertaken on different days. No February bear spread was available January 18, just as none was there on January 22, hence we held the same spread in duplicate, so to speak, and would prove nothing unless we ended them on different dates. That was the point of the exercise.

In holding on to the bear spread we violated our rule; take any decent profit—free translation, take any 3 or 4 point profit. So we were in uncharted waters.

Little transpired on the next day. Tuesday, January 30, saw the OEX drop 2 points to trade in a range of about 6. The spread was between 3 7/8 and 4 1/4 throughout the day.

The spread worked out in the morning on January 30, when the Dow was down about 35 points and the OEX was around 300. So this spread was cashed in at 5 points. Since the initial cost was 1 3/4 our profit was 3 1/4, or $1,625 minus commissions. You could double the number of contracts, quadruple them, the sky, your wallet and nerve are the limits.

The extra trade required the same margin, $5,000, as the concurrent one. Nothing was saved there.

The exercise turned out to be pointless but not valueless; on the contrary, it wound up with more profit than the competing bear spread so it wasn't a duplicate. You could argue, of course, that if we had held on to the competing bear spread long enough, that one also would have been completely profitable. But the courage to hold on arose mostly because we already had a profit in our pocket and felt more inclined to take added risk. So, the chief value, once past the extra dough, turned out to be psychological. This doesn't alter the fact that the market doesn't cooperate with good intentions or bad, unless they are illegal, when its cooperation can become very expensive (see Ivan Boesky).

A good market player is one with a plan and a strategy. It isn't enough to master (say) the vertical spreads of Strategy One. If the market goes against you, i.e., runs over one leg of your strategy, forcing you to extricate it and establish a new one, your spread is not profitable. At best, profit has been postponed, which means unprofitable use of money and time. At worst, you take a loss on the assumption that you chose the wrong instrument and need to move to the right one, the one that reflects the new market situation, that being the reason for giving up on the vertical spread. Thus, you would now go either to a bull or bear spread, a bull AND bear spread, or simply buy puts or calls or, finally, stand aside. These are not, of course, the only alternatives, but they do cover much of the OEX waterfront.

Throughout these chapters you read that we had other positions simultaneous with the one under discussion, not all of which we run down concurrently. That is what we are trying to convey with the phrase alternate strategy. Ultimately, what is advocated is the correct mix of all the strategies undertaken in this book, though the selling of combinations in Strategy III is advocated only for veteran traders with deep pockets and a track record, or others who hedge with the correct buying strategies simultaneously.

Update

Let us come far forward in time to 1994, when the U.S. economy was growing despite the huge Clinton tax increase of 1993, the equivalent of which had sent George Bush to his doom in 1992. The U.S. Congress was struggling with the health care debate in which the left-wing of the Clinton Administration, led by Clinton himself, sought to expand health coverage under federal administration to about 100 million souls, which Clinton generously extended to Republicans, defining their souls to fall within his guidelines.

Markets had fallen from early February to suspenseful April lows. The Dow Jones Industrials had dropped from 4000 intraday down to about 3525 intraday at April Fool's Day. The transportation stocks made their lows around 1530 later on in April, around the 17th. The utilities, which had been in a bear market since Christmas of 1993, had rallied briefly in April, then took another slow plunge beginning around the last week in April and continuing, month after month. That was considered a certain sign by market technicians that we were either in a bear market or about to enter its portals. The errant utilities, following their own doom and gloom scenario, were a divergence from the industrials and the transportations. Remember, the Dow is made of up three separate, radically unequal branches of industrials, transportations and utilities, with the utilities the slowest to move, in perverse consequence having the reputation as the prima donnas of the three.

The divergence of the three components of the Dow was not constant. But overall it was drastic. Until May 1994, the three averages were more or less in sync, but beginning about that time the industrials and transportations began a move upwards that was not joined by the utilities. That's where the real divergence arose. Technicians pounced on that phase to issue portentous announcements of doom.

In retrospect the doom that ensued was not terminal. The bond market continued to hem and haw, as if seeking forgiveness for past sins but refusing to guarantee a spotless future. At least, the worst of it seemed over.

Not according to the OEX. The bull spread opportunities in late September 1994 were flashing no go signals. A bear spread turned green. On September 27, we dipped into the bear hive; bought a 435 Oct put, sold a 425 Oct put for a spread of 2. The OEX was at 428. The Dow, which had been sliding, was at 3849. It made its first gain on this day in weeks. We didn't think this was the start of any juicy rally.

Anyone sleeping through the last four years or more would have been jolted by the new cost figures of this spread. Though the ratios were similar to those of the past, the dollar numbers were higher. We bought five puts for 6 1/8, sold 5 puts for 4 1/8. It cost $3,062.50 to buy; we took in $2,062.50 on the sale. So we entered with a loss of 1 grand. That wasn't untypical of trading in the beloved past.

The bear changed its colors thereupon, acting like a bull, sending us into the state of catatonia (sometimes called California). For two days it went up, then reversed to the desired direction, dropping back a few points. On October 4 the bear changed its spots from bull to bear once again; the OEX took a nosedive to 420.50 (the Dow dropped over 45 points to 3801).

Now the puts we bought for 6 1/8 were at 15 1/4, the puts we sold for 4 1/8 were at 7 3/8. We have noted that a move of 45 Dow points often will make a spread work perfectly. This was more than perfect. We sold back the puts we bought for $7625. We bought back the puts we sold for $3,687.50. The quick profit was $3,937.50. It was on five contracts. Suppose you had 20 or 40? With 20 you pocket $15,750. With 40 double that to $31,500. Margin requirements would vary but could be as high as $50,000 for 40 contracts. But that's your money. It was undisturbed. You can see it as a $31,500 profit on a $50,000 investment in about a week. You could afford to do that 52 weeks out of the year.

Two things about this trade; it was risky. Suppose you had used 20 or 40 contracts and the market had gone against you. The losses could have been equal to the profits—$15,000 to $30,000. Whenever you use this kind of strategy you must hedge, buying calls in a bear spread, puts in a bull.

The second thing to notice is that again the rule of this spread—buy the in-the-money option closest to the current index, sell the out-of-the-money closest to the index—was violated. We used a spread of 10 points instead of the usual five in our quest for a usable (profitable) deal. The five extra points gave us a spread of 2 (difference between 6 1/8 bought, 4 1/8 sold), which is about the best you can expect. We were lucky quickly; the market went up a few days but then swooned into our arms. The market is fickle; you need to play all the angles as they appear. The mathematics of the trade were simple enough. As the market dropped, the option we bought expanded far more quickly than the one we sold. It (the bought option) was in the money, hence it expanded instantly to every downward move. The sold option expanded much less quickly. It was out-of-the-money.

Because movements of this sort are increasingly common in a market trading around 4,000 (Dow), spreads of this sort are increasingly able to generate quick profits (or losses). That is why you must hedge. The two ways of hedging are simply to buy options on the opposite side of your spread. If you own a bull spread, you should buy OEX puts. If a bear, buy calls. Or, put on an opposing spread. With increasing volatility, if you give yourself enough time before expiration date, you have the chance of winning with both a bull and bear spread. Meanwhile, you are fully hedged. Moreover, since the advent of collars on the NYSE, there have been no more "blowouts" such as those of 1987 and 1989. They happened because of program trading and panic. The collars cut off such trading at 50 points up or down. Nobody panics nowadays at a 50 point gain or loss, but you can panic all the way to the bank with profits as shown above.

The huge drops in 1987 and 1989 would have caused catastrophic losses in any unhedged option (or stock) position. But if you had both a bull and bear spread in those times you would have had enormous gains on your bear spread balanced by enormous losses in the bull. But, suppose you had the sense to take profits on the bear spread and hold the bull? Since the market came back about two-thirds of the way you would have held on to about two-thirds of your huge profits (canceling out all the losses).

Strategy Three: Combinations

In the old days (1 B.C.—before the crash) the selling of combinations was an exhilirating (risky) but profitable way to do OEX options. No more. Many people lost more money than they could afford in the crash, and brokers stopped using them, or erected barriers of $100,000 in margin costs to discourage all but the high rollers.

The strategy remains dangerous and expensive, given the propensity of computer trading and risk arbitrage to send the market scooting away from you without warning or hint. So this strategy, and the use of the S&P 500 stock index futures are not for the faint of heart or those who cannot bear to lose money, even in an eventual winning cause.

To generalize about the new use of OEX combination selling, it is to be undertaken only AFTER a huge market move, a crisis. One uses OEX combination selling only occasionally, now. One uses it with hedges, and at the very least the buying of puts in tandem with the selling of combinations. It is not enough to balance off the selling of combinations with a bear spread. Bear and bull spreads have only a limited hedging role, whereas in today's markets you need the absolute hedging range of puts bought in tandem. In theory one should be able to leave any losing OEX trade; but we learned in the crash that if the phone won't ring at your broker's desk there is no limit to loss except the buying of puts. To be sure, we are promised that there will be no replay of the crash in respect to unanswered phones; technology is now in place to prevent it. Promises, promises.

Is there any value in studying trades from the fall of 1986? They have the same exemplary value as the trades in your morning paper today. The same relationships prevail today; you may even gain a bit of added insight by comparing the trades that interest you now with those that happened over three years ago. Both market technicians and traditionalists agree that market cycles exist along with business and other cycles, so it makes sense to study the past if you think it is possible to illuminate

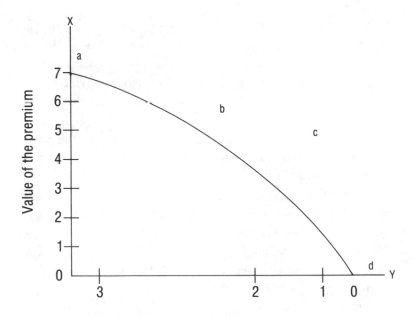

This shows an approximation of time decay by an OEX option. The option's value is represented by the vertical line X, the time remaining to expiration is shown in months along the line Y. The curve (a, b, c, d) reflects an option premium ideal for combination writing—i.e., where little action has occurred in the market. The curve would look very different in a highly volatile market. All else being equal, however, the curve of an option approaching expiration, whose time value has not been altered drastically by big moves in the Dow, will look like the curve in this graph, especially in the last few weeks. The premium values on the left often are exceeded, but just as often are less than the numbers shown (0 to $7).

the present. In any case, the past is all we have to study, unless we are into witchcraft. I once knew an options "expert" who refused to recommend any options book because, as he put it, "books are about the past." But it did not prevent him from charging large fees to lecture about options and to issue guidebooks that were full of blanks he filled in at the lectures. These took the form of "if the market does this then these options will do that," as if the market is a kind of medicine that you take in order to obtain certain specific benefits, or that it is a machine that can be wound up to do controllable movements. It is neither; what is predictable about it is that it is always difficult and potentially treacherous, and that is why elaborate hedging tactics are constantly necessary. That is why it is also essential to study as much of its workings as possible.

Favorable Market

On September 11, 1986, the market dropped a record 86 Dow points, and another 34 points or so the next day. It moved around 1740 for the next week and then began another strong move upward. That's when we entered, believing that the market would enter a new trading range with wide swings. On September 25 the market moved downward, dropping the OEX almost 5 points. The 235 call dropped to 1 11/16 from 2 1/2, the 210 put went up from 2 3/8 to 3 1/2. The position was in no danger of margin calls; the 210–235 channel was far away from the OEX close of 219. On September 29 the OEX dropped to 218. The Nov 235 call was now 1 3/8, down from 2 1/2. The 210 put was at 3 5/8, up from 2 3/8. We might have been tempted to take a profit by cashing in on the call side, which would have given us $500 (on five contracts) more or less, but it would have left us with an uncovered put option now increased by more than a total of $500. (It had gone up from 1 2/8). We are not in the risky business of selling uncovered options, which have unlimited potential for loss. So we resisted. There are times, in option trading, when one must remember Oscar Wilde's "I can resist everything except temptation" and resist it.

In the week now finished we could see potential for profit as well as loss. Still, the channel was intact, the market far away from the closest concern, the put increasing in value for the buyer but not for the seller. Market volume, always a barometer of volatility, had leveled off in the 120 million share daily range.

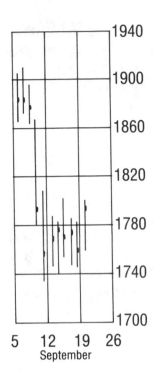

This chart shows the two day drops in the Dow September 11 and 12 when it moved from about 1870 down to about 1780 on September 11, and moved another 65 points intraday on September 12 (from high point to low point). The total loss on the two days was 155 points, but overlapping and recovery from the lows cut that number to around 130. But options were being exposed to the losses and you could have had losses reflected in the full 155 points if you had reacted nervously and at the wrong time.

The market next commenced moving up, with the OEX closing at about 222 on October 2. The 235 call was now at 2 1/8, the 210 put was at 2 9/16. So the original position was more or less intact—originally the call was at 2 1/2, the put at 2 3/8. But we had gained valuable time—valuable in that the market had gone nowhere. This is the optimum thing it can do for us, since our ideal goal is that the options we have sold will expire worthless, which they do when they remain within the channel we have entered, the 210–235 OEX channel, allowing us to keep the entire premium of about $2,400.

Two weeks later, on October 15, the market moved upward, taking the OEX up almost 4 points to 225.34. Here the 235 call was at 1 5/8, the 210 put at 1 1/16. Now we had a profit on both sides of the combo, about three weeks after opening it—7/8 on the call and 1 1/16 on the put, for a total of

1 15/16, almost 2, or 1/16 shy of $1,000 on five contracts. Cashing in the contract after three weeks would make a good profit even after a commission, bringing it down in the $900 area. But faint heart never won so let's take it further.

A week later, October 22, it looked like this: the 235 call was at 9/16, the 210 put at 7/8, the OEX index now at 222.95 or almost exactly where we commenced it, at 223. Now we do have a good profit, a month after we commenced. Cashing in would have given us 1 15/16 profit on the call, and 1 1/4 on the put, or about $1,750 on the $5,000 investment (margin). That is on the basis of one month's time. If you want to annualize it that comes out to $21,000. Using ten contracts doubles it, and ten contracts differ only in that you need another $5,000 in margin up front (stock certificates, and so forth).

But wait, let's go on with the trade. The market, more or less neutral until now, suddenly came to life. On November 3, or three weeks away from expiration, the OEX index closed at about 232. Our combo now looked like this: the 235 Nov call was at 1 7/16 (2 1/2 originally), the Nov 210 put was at 1/8 (2 3/8 originally). So things are clouded. The put has given the combo a gain of 2 1/4; the call (with a net loss of 1/2) has given us a gain of 1 1/16. We are ahead by 3 5/16, or $1,593.75.

The market had a sizeable buildup in volume leading to the movement upward, then it dropped back into the 120 plus million share days that had characterized it the past several months. So things continued to look rosy.

They got even rosier. The OEX remained around 232 and then on November 13, dropped almost 4 points to 228. Here we were, eight days from expiration—November 21. The numbers gave us this go-go profile of our combo: the 235 call was now at 3/16; the 210 put was at 1/16. We were within 1/4 of total victory—$2,438.00. The total time was almost eight weeks. The next week—expiration—was more of the same. The OEX expired blissfully, ending around 235, or about 11 points higher than the initial purchase level of 223. So holding it the final week to expiration would have given you the complete total of about $2,437.50, from which you subtract commissions (about $100). Nine weeks had passed, with few nervous episodes.

Notice that when we sold the original contract, we were betting that for the 235 call to become risky the market would have to move up from OEX 223 to OEX 235, (12 OEX points). That means the Dow would have had to move up 12 times 7, since it takes 7 Dow points to equal 1 of the OEX, usually, for a total of 84 points. The Dow actually went up more than that briefly, from the 1794 area on September 22, to 1890 on November 3, to 1902 on November 5, to a high of 1907, intraday on November 6, closing at 1891. But the OEX did not carry through, going up on that day to a high of 232.87—dangerously close to the 235 upper limit that would have triggered a margin call, probably. (Ask your broker about such matters because wide differences arise.) But the ratio didn't prevail; the OEX trailed the Dow. It often does. What does this say?

Our combo, which returned about $2,400 (minus commissions) in nine weeks on margin of $5,000, is a scenario of real trades. Plenty of people invested far more on margin and had correspondingly richer returns. In fact, a beginner could have done well, getting some toes wet, with a single contract, turning in a profit of better than $400 on $1,000 of margin. By contrast, a ten-contract lot, on $10,000 margin, which is probably the most common size among traders, returned over $4,850, (minus commissions) in the nine weeks.

The first thing the trade says is that a lot of money can be made. But it's only one of the strategies we employ. Also, there is always an element of luck in trying to time the market, which is what we're doing. Our approach to market timing and the OEX, if followed more or less scrupulously, will be sufficient, as we will see in the buying strategy section.

Stop-Loss Parameters

When you sell option combinations (puts and calls), there are several ways to approach loss limitation. The first is to take a loss of no more than 40 percent of your potential profit. That means you must buy back the losing side of the combination you sell. If your potential profit is $1,200 on a five-contract combination, buy back the losing side when it is about $500 in the red. Given the vagaries of transaction time and market rush (plus commission costs) it should be possible to hold losses around the $100 per contract area.

The reason you have lost money on one side of the combination is that the market has moved rapidly in the direction of that side. Part of the loss will be covered by the gain on the other side. The tactic to recover some of the losing side loss is to buy back that option and wait a couple of days until the market settles down. Big moves are always caused by big volume. Study the volume figures surrounding the big move, and when they return to the numbers typical of the period in which you sold the options, resell the losing side. This will not recover all the premium you received the first time, but it will get you back into the black—recouping your $500 or more loss. Meanwhile, the winning side will help keep you in the black.

The next way to approach loss control is to take the loss, take the profit on the winning side, which won't be nearly enough to put the total into the black, and then initiate a spread strategy.

If you want a quick recovery—you should buy options in the direction of the losing side, if lively market movement continues in big volume.

Usually the correct procedure is to buy both a put and a call. Even though the market may appear to be moving irresistibly in one direction, you don't want to take any chances of a loss. You will, of course, lose money on the side that is not favored by the market, but the loss will be the cost of that option. Meanwhile, if the other winning side continues its big move it will rapidly make enough money to restore whatever losses you suffered

Stop-Loss Parameters (continued)

originally from the combination you sold, and will usually give you an adequate profit.

Even on the famous 86 point drop in the Dow, September 11, 1986, you could have used the strategy of buying back the losing side (the put) and then restored a winning position. The market began to drop at the opening of the bell and within a short time had lost 20 points. All the pressures were on the selling side and it was clear that the market was in for a drastic loss. Anyone holding a combination could have gotten out with a loss of 1 or 2 points ($100 or $200 per contract). Because the indicators continued to show a sharply lower market the next day, it was no time to reestablish the position. But two days later the huge volume disappeared and the market was back into a trading pattern. At that point you could have sold another put (assuming you still had the call) and your profitable combination would have been back in place.

Finally, an aggressive trader would have used our least discussed strategy, thus far: the S&P 500 stock index futures contract, with which he would have added a bundle. But that strategy comes at the end of this book.

The key to a loss is to accept it gracefully. Losses are inevitable, but they can be countered with a strategy as above.

Unfavorable Market Action

Everything went right in the trades above. Now let's talk about a trade that went wrong—almost. It shows the problems in avoiding peril.

On September 11, 1986, the market made its largest drop in history, in terms of points (but not percentage; that happened in 1929), dropping 86 points. (It was soon to surpass that drop.) Anyone holding an OEX combination on that day would have been astonished and perhaps frightened at the speed of the decline. Though such a drop was unprecedented and not likely to occur often, it proceeded to happen again, and perhaps

	9/16	9/29	10/2	10/15	10/22	11/3	11/13	11/13	11/21
CALL PREMIUM	2½	1¹¹/₁₆	1³/₈	2⅛	1¹/₁₆	1⅝	9/16	3/16	0
PUT PREMIUM	2⅜	3½	3⅝	2⁹/₁₆	1¹/₁₆	⅞	⅛	1/16	0
OEX INDEX	223	219	218	222	225.34	222.95	232	228	234
CHANNEL 25 PTS.									
DATES	9/16	9/29	10/2	10/15	10/22	11/3	11/13	11/13	11/21

History of completely successful combination showing those dates and prices when the market made strong moves, some of which were threatening (when the index approached 235).

it will become fairly common when the market gets above 3000 or thereabouts. Then, a 5 percent drop would be 150 points, and a 2 1/2 percent drop would be 75 points. Such drops can be expected often in the age of computer trading.

Computer programs that are triggered by specific drops or rises have already become familiar. Their signs are fairly easily discerned. On September 11 it was perfectly clear by 9:30 a.m. that the market would experience a sweeping downward movement. Buying was almost totally missing; the trading was heavy and big trades were dominating continuously. The preponderance of selling over buying was fixed almost from the start, with an almost 10 to 1 ratio. It expanded to 12 to 1 and more. Not until late in the trading day did some slight buying occur, but the basic pattern never changed. All other short-time market indicators were shouting "sell."

For our purposes the indicators most relevant to short-term movements begin with volume. On September 11 the volume was record setting from the start. But one important sign to note was the volume on preceding days. A volume buildup had started September 3 and built up sharply through September 5, then dropped back September 8 to the 10. The eruption of the next three days, beginning with the huge drop on September 11, was record setting. Big volume almost always causes big market moves.

The advance/decline line (number of stocks advancing versus number declining) is equally vital with volume. These two indicators are virtually all anyone needs for the OEX, in short-term trading. But one should also look at the TRIN, which reflects market direction and force. When the TRIN is above 1.00 the market is bearish, but more importantly, the TRIN must be below .75 and dropping for the market to move up quickly. On the days in question it was down in the .20s, as low as it gets, and it remained there. Remember, the most important initial thing about the TRIN is its direction. Once that is established, you look at the number.

Anyone holding a combination on September 11, 1986, probably would have entered it with the market around Dow 1875. Suppose the combination was in a 25 point channel, based on an OEX 230, with a call at 245, a put at 220—real numbers at that time with the Dow around 1875.

Why would a speculator have been in the market at that precise time? One aspect of damage control—which is another name for hedging—is to determine the right place to sell OEX combinations. One never sells them in a market that is in the middle of an emphatic up or down trend. One always waits until the dust settles. In trending markets you buy combinations (Strategy Three), or you put on spreads (Strategy Two), or you do both. The market, throughout August of 1986, was on a move almost straight up, from 1740 to 1900. It arrived at the 1875 area about August 20. There it paused to trade back and forth, which is exactly the type of market behavior that favors selling OEX combinations. One should never enter any other kind of market to sell a combo.

Trading back and forth, beginning August 20, set the stage for selling a combo, based on an OEX index around 230, with a call at 245 and a put at 220. We deliberately spaced the channel so that there would be more room on the up side (the call) because market bias on August 20 appeared to be upward, based on our indicators. So, figuring 7 Dow points for 1 OEX point, the market would have to travel 105 points up to Dow 1980 before entering margin call territory (loss), or 70 points down to Dow 1805 before entering losing territory.

The combo had only been trading fifteen days when the September 11 and 12 disaster hit, but it was already profitable, and many less aggressive traders might have been tempted to take the roughly $1,000 profit available (on five contracts) just before September 11. Signs were developing to suggest prudent profit taking. In the last week of August the market dropped on declining volume, then spurted sharply up in volume into the 180 million-share range as it moved into September, sending the Dow up briefly (intraday) to an all-time high close to 1940. The high volatility in this period saw the market rushing up and down, almost directionless. There were many divergences and non-confirmations from utilities and OTC markets, with the advance/decline line showing far fewer advances over declines than in earlier big rallies, and no discernible market leadership developing from stock groups that were usual leaders, like IBM and GM. These troubling signs indicated that anything could happen and it did—the big egg the market laid on September 11.

Cautious speculators might have gotten out of the market the day before, and some market timing services warned subscribers to sell. Many market watchers noted the weaknesses and contradictions in the market. But most people, and in particular those speculators involved in combinations (us), would have looked at the numbers and decided that there was "nothing to fear but fear itself."

That would have been a mistake, correctible as follows. We have already noted that by 9:30, certainly by 10:00 a.m., all the bells were ringing, if you were listening, warning of ogres—severe market decline. At that point and certainly later with no sign of recovery at the usual daily trading nexus of 11:00 or 11:30 when some counter move, however feeble, usually pokes its head up, anyone with the right knowledge would have bought back the puts. They were dangerously inflated but you could have bought them back for a loss of about one point over what you received for them (about 1 3/4, depending on the day and time you sold them) for a loss of $500 to $750 or $1,000 at most for five contracts. That is our prescribed stop-loss point.

Having done that, the next thing to do would have been to buy as many puts as you considered expedient. These would have redeemed your losses, especially if you held them through the next day's loss of another 30 plus points on the

Dow. They would, in fact, have put you back into a profitable position, especially as the calls were down considerably, offsetting in value (to you) some of your losses on the puts.

The third thing to do was to put on a bear spread (Strategy Two). That also would have become profitable over the next two trading days. Next, and this requires a commodity trading account, you could have sold an S&P 500 stock index futures contract, or two or three (see the last section of this book).

The final damage control step to take would have been to judge the market on the third day of the sequence, and perhaps the fourth and fifth, waiting for the market to settle and reestablish your combination by selling the new appropriate put—10 points lower or thereabouts. That would have almost completely nullified your loss by itself. Meanwhile you would have had two other profit centers working for you: the puts you bought and the spread you entered, to say nothing of the S&P 500 stock index futures contract that works perfectly in this situation. So, what started out as an apparent disaster—a large loss—wound up as an especially large profit, because the market was giving off unambiguous signals, in effect begging you to take appropriate action. Once such a market commences—whether up or down—and you can expect such markets increasingly in computer-traded markets, you will find many occasions throughout the year for stunning results. With knowledge and practice you won't get sentimentally attached to your latest trade, and you will cash it in at the right time. It's a psychological as well as a logical procedure, and both require learning. The fact that it sometimes demands contrary psychology is another branch of the same learning tree; veteran investors and speculators know the value of contrary thinking.

A New Trade

Having turned a potential disaster into a handsome profit by employing several strategies in tandem, and having waited out a highly profitable combination whose members expired worthless, thus enriching us to the tune of $2,437.50 (minus commissions), we turned next to a new position.

One of the keys to OEX trading is that you do not let sleeping dogs or beauties lie there but leap over them into a new trade. On November 24, the Dow began a 10 point move up, eventually reaching almost 25 points above its opening and finally closing about 13 points up for the day. Early on, volume wasn't high enough to assert a trend, so we assumed that selling a new combination was in order (no trend, *sell; buy* the OEX in a trending market). We sold five combinations around noon, when the market was up about 10, the OEX at 235. A 20 point channel offered a Jan 245 call at 1 3/4, a 225 Jan put at 2 1/4. Since the market had been moving up beginning the previous three sessions, doing so with strength, it was risky to sell combinations only 12 points above the previous day's close, especially as the entry point we chose was 3 points above the day's opening OEX level. In effect, that meant that we were betting the market wouldn't continue its rise of the previous three sessions, but would settle into a trading range pattern. In a situation of this sort, market direction and movement are vital to assess. If the market was not settling into a trading range after the three day rise, but was about to get up steam for another sharp eruption upward, the upper channel would soon be overrun. What about putting on a bull spread? Wouldn't that be the strategy of preference? In fact, given the shape of market movement going all the way back to April 1986, when the market had been in a widely swinging trading range, it made perfect sense to use both strategies—a combination and a bull spread.

Let's follow the combination (the bull spread is in the chapter devoted to spreads).

Because the market had been in a trading range for so long interrupted mostly by the huge two day move in September and earlier moves up and down of consequence, one needed to be cautious, fearful of another Vesuvius eruption. We resolved to take profits early on the new combination, if they presented themselves, rather than risk sweating out the entire time period. Better to take those profits you have than wait for those you know not of, to introduce paraphrase into speculation. It is the first cautionary move in combinations but not the only ones, as we will see.

We therefore sold the Jan 245 call at 1 3/4, the 225 Jan put at 2 1/4, a total of 4 ($400) times five contracts which equals $2,000, with margin requirement of about $5,000.

The next day we were somewhat startled to see the call up to 2 3/16 but pleased to observe the decline of the put to 1 7/8. More or less a balancing out—though not quite—as the market gained 6 points. More important was the increase in volume— call volume went up substantially, while put volume declined. This was a warning that the market might be readying a rally. It was also an opportunity for our bull spread. On November 26 the 225 Jan put declined slightly to 1 13/16, the Jan 245 call remained at 2 3/16.

The market remained stationary the next day, but the call declined while the put gained, resulting in another standoff.

On December 2 the market surged 20 points very quickly with the OEX moving in step, up over 3 points, and sending the call price up sharply. This bad news was immediate good news for our bull spread, which was making up the paper loss in the combination. We did nothing, despite the OEX close of 240.95, which was up almost 5 points from the day before, as the Dow moved up 43 points.

The combination looked like this when the smoke cleared: the 225 put was down to 1 3/16, which was good news: the 245 Jan call was 3 1/2, which was bad (we sold it initially for 1 3/4, which means we had a paper loss of 1 3/4 per contract or $875 total). Meanwhile, the bull spread was actually showing a higher paper profit.

What, you may wonder, were the metaphysics of the bull spread instead of, say, a bear spread? It was a market call; we had a bull market that we judged to have much life remaining in it, based on our assessment of the economy and expert economic opinion. We believe that markets reflect the realities of the economy; if they did not it would be too bizarre to contemplate. It would mean that all the market transactions involving U.S. economic activity were random, accidental or purely mechanical, having little relation to what lie behind them. The market had been trading back and forth for months, with a few corrections here and there, sufficient we believed to view it as oversold and ready for a new push upward. If we thought the new push was destined to be galvanic and imme- diate we would have avoided selling the combination and, instead, would have bought a combination along with the bull spread. But we didn't reckon with yet another huge leap upward, such as occurred in January 1987.

Meanwhile, we judged the next day to be crucial; if the market continued an upward sweep it would be necessary to buy back the call and then buy an OEX call (five contracts) on the assumption that the market was again in an upward trend. But December 3 dawned uncertainly, an upward swing of 12 points, then a downward move into much volatile trading back and forth. On the day the OEX gained a mere .05—nothing to worry about at the end but a lot of worry intraday. It now stood at 241; the call stood at 3 3/4, the put at 1 1/8. The next day brought even better news; the Dow again went nowhere, and the OEX lost 1.13, putting the Jan 245 call at 3 7/8, the 225 put at 1 1/8. The call price continued to show an upward bias, disconcerting but not alarming. Remember also that expiration day, now becoming a high holy day for OEX players, is the third Friday of January for us and we are only in December, weeks away. We violated our own advice in a way—to sell five week-out combinations not seven week-outs as we did, and if none is worth the selling, due to insufficiently rich premiums, wait until the numbers come around, as they will. On December 5 the call price receded to 3; the put moved up slightly to 1 7/16. Nothing to be alarmed over.

The next trading day, December 8, yielded another directionless market, the OEX closing at 238.67, a gain of .60, the Jan 245 call closing at 3 1/8 and the 225 put closing at 1 1/4. The market story was the same the next three days. On Friday the OEX had dropped back to 235.40, where we entered it. The 245 call was now at 1 5/8, the 225 put at 1 11/16. Progress, but not enough to take profit.

The market approached Christmas week, inducing some nervousness over the rhetoric about a Christmas rally. We did not want Santa to dump this in our market basket too generously, though the possession of the bull spread tore our emotions in half.

Little was happening, once past the department store windows, to enliven the first part of the Christmas week. Nothing ever did happen. On December 24 the OEX gained .52, sitting at 235.80. In other words it had behaved perfectly; on balance it had gone nowhere since we bought it back in November. The 245 call was 15/16, the 225 put was 1/2. Now we had a tidy profit, lo and behold, and the question of scowling all the way to the bank had arisen. We held out; greed overcame reason.

The market remained calm for the next few days. On December 29 the OEX dropped 2.20 points, the 245 call was at 3/8, the 225 put was 3/4. We decided to cash in our chips, remembering our resolution, spurred on by our belief that the market was in basically sound condition, hence possibly preparing for a rally. Several of our favorite market timers were declaring such a state to be imminent. We had sold the combination for $2,000 (five contracts). When we bought it back at $112.50 (1 1/8), our profit was $1,437.50 ($287.50 per contract), minus commissions, on a margin investment of $5,000 in a period of about five weeks. We also made a profit on our bull spread.

Anyone confident of the ability to work the OEX by now is asking, "Why limit yourself to five contracts?" This is a popular question. In fact, ten contracts are the usual number, and some investor-speculators do many more. But I am addressing the people, not the millionaires, in an effort to make millionaires out of the people.

The combination we have just walked through was done with virtually no anxieties. There were only a few isolated moments, but so there are when you cross any busy street intersection. Anxiety in investing must be mastered; there are no pills.

Had we waited one more day the combination would have produced extra dollars. The market dropped on December 30, the OEX closed at 232.75 with the Jan 245 call at 5/16 and the 225 put at 11/16, for a total of 1, instead of the 1 1/8 price tag that we cashed in. As it happened, discretion was indeed the better part of valor. The market turned on the power on January 2, 1987, and went on an almost unprecedented rampage, moving from about 1920 to over 2400 in record time, making combination selling in the OEX a disaster area but making bull spreads and the buying of OEX options an utterly blissful activity, to say nothing of buying the S&P 500 stock index futures!

On January 2, 1987, the Dow started at 1900.59. At day's end it was up 31.36, which was a fair day's work but not unusual. Had you held on to the combination (Jan 235) you would have continued to make more money, since the call was at 7/16 and the put was at 5/16 for a total of 12/16 or 3/4.

Indeed, on Monday, January 5, we were tempted to go back into a combination, which we did, following Oscar Wilde, whose "I can resist everything except temptation" is the speculator's truest epigram, for better or worse. We sold the Feb 250 call at 1 7/8, the 230 Feb put at 1 11/16 for a total of 3 9/16. Five contracts at 3 9/16 comes out to around $1,800 with commissions (my broker; yours will be different).

The next day, embarked on this six-week odyssey (again, not the most desired five-week span), the market finished up about 3 1/2 Dow points, the OEX, little changed, up .27. This story was repeated the next day, January 7, with a close that advanced the OEX 1.96 points. The Feb 250 call went to 2, the 230 put declined to 1 3/8—a standoff.

The market was now clearly in a strong move upwards, having advanced from the 1900 area up to the 2000 and above area in the period from January 2 to the 9. This posed a dilemma. We were again in a tandem bull spread (see appropriate chapter) which was showing good results quickly—a sign of underlying bullishness but by no means conclusive evidence. Yet the OEX had not yet approached the danger point—the upward limit of 250. January 8, a cold day in Chicago for combination sellers, sent the OEX up to 242, in an advance of 1.15. More ominous was the close of the Dow at 2002.25, which suggested more upward movement ahead—the breaching of the resistance point of 2000. The Feb 250 call, which we sold at 1 7/8, was now at 2 3/16, the 230 put, sold at 11/16, was at 1 1/8, meaning that we were losing at *both* ends of the combination. How can that happen? As we've noted, the OEX is a weighted index and when one of the heavyweights like IBM or GM moves apart from the trend, the index is distorted. The 7 point move that usually translates into a 1 point move in the OEX, translates either more or less than that. It's like the gorilla that sits where it pleases.

More of the same ensued on January 9, 1987, with the Dow moving up 3.66, but well off its high for the day. The OEX closed at 245.45, not yet in danger territory, but just a few points away. The 250 call was now at 2 3/4, the 230 put at 7/8.

The OEX lacked even the grace to offer us a profit on the put, despite the clear movement upwards. Our anxiety, which had risen sharply during the day when the Dow reached its high point near 2012, from whence it backed off to 2005.91, abated somewhat. It was not aided by the fact that volume had picked up and was beginning to surge, approaching, in a rising pattern, the 200 million share level.

Volume slacked off Monday, January 12, but the market continued its pattern of advances in small increments. The OEX closed at 246.67, the 250 call was at 3, the 230 put at 5/8. We were in a losing position, but was it a lost cause? That is the question, as Hamlet said.

Not overall. We had another bull spread going on at the same time, which was working perfectly, and we were contemplating the idea of buying OEX calls. We were also toying with the idea of quitting the combination play and taking our losses.

We did none of those things on that day, procrastinating for the usual reasons—sloth and fear of the unknown.

January 13 brought a reprieve. The OEX closed down slightly, even though the Dow moved up 3.52 to 2012.94. The OEX now stood at 245.75, with the combination in fairly good shape—the 250 call at 2 3/4, the 230 put at 5/8. It was losing but not as much.

Drastic Action

We were in hot water the next day, sufficient enough to take drastic action. The market began to move up sharply on heavy volume early in the session. The OEX spurted up; we decided to get out of the losing call position. We took our lumps, buying back the five calls at 3, which cost $1,500. But we kept the put positions, which would cut the loss in half, eventually.

We then bought five calls for the same $1,500, and a single S&P 500 stock index futures contract, which required $6,000 on margin, separate from the OEX requirement.

Our bull spread was countering the loss from the call side of the combination. So, despite the market going against us, our overall strategy was in the black. Notice that we did not wait until the market overwhelmed the combination trade. We watched it closely, deciding that the upward rush of the market was not slowing but gaining in intensity—in eight previous trading days the market had advanced about 100 points on increasing volume. The transportation and utilities indexes were also advancing steadily. Other indicators like the advance/decline numbers were bullish; every sign pointed upwards despite the absence of any unusual signs from the economy or indeed from world markets. It may seem a far cry from trading options to the state of the world economy, but automation relates markets more intimately to each other than before.

Some traders, faced with the loss we experienced, would do nothing, hoping for the best, confident that the market would turn in their favor sooner or later. We've done it. But that is a prescription for disaster; markets have a lordly indifference to your fate or prognostications.

On January 15 the OEX leaped another 3.47, the Dow jumped almost 36 points. We were out of the combination on the call side, but we still owned a now naked put—a 230 Feb that we had sold for 1 11/16. The put was now 7/16, which meant that it was getting close to cutting half our loss on the call side. We decided to hold on, especially since everything else was working well—the OEX calls we bought, the bull spread and the S&P 500 stock index futures contract.

The stunning volatility of the market in January raised the questions: What is going on here? Are combinations being destroyed? Is this another case of a good thing that everyone is learning about and thus chasing away?

What's going on is computer trading. The market is increasingly robotized. Computer programs, based largely on the S&P 500 stock index futures, dictate buying and selling either the stocks or the stock index futures, depending on whether the cash price of the S&P 500 is above or below the futures price. When the cash price is much below the futures price (and these ratios are determined by computer programs) the equity markets go up as buying programs of stocks arc turned on. When the futures price drops below today's cash price of the S&P 500 index, sell programs are instituted. It's mechanical and automatic. It plays the devil with the best laid plans of mice and men. It turns to mush the most arcane deliberations. Trading in the stock market is overwhelmingly done by pension, mutual and other big fund managers, as well as by overseas fund managers. Predicting what they will do is impossible because of the zombie aspect. Is it fatal to all deliberation about markets? It makes markets more difficult but not necessarily impossible to understand.

After puzzling over the dilemma of the combination problem, it became clear that the best strategy was the one we were using—buying the OEX and buying an S&P 500 stock index futures contract, and using a wider channel for the OEX combination play. Instead of a 20 point margin—10 above and 10 below—we would use a 25 or 30 point margin, larger when available.

Red Letter Day

January 23 was a red letter day. The market had a volume of just over 300 million shares and a range that spanned from about 2060 to over 2200, or more than 140 points up and down, finishing 44 points down. The OEX covered over 13 points, from a high of 270.93 to a low of 257.32 and a close of 259.01, leaving it in negative territory to the tune of 4.47 points. It was one of those rare days when the only good strategy was no strategy—when being out of the options and futures markets was the only rational policy. But if you were trapped in such a day and couldn't get through to your broker, because of the

Chicago Board 1/23/87

S&P 100 INDEX

Strike	Calls—Last			Puts—Last		
Price	Feb	Mar	Apr	Feb	Mar	Apr
210	59	....	....	1/16	1/8	....
215	51 1/2	53 1/2	....	1/16	1/8	....
220	....	52	....	1/16	3/16	....
225	34	44	43	1/8	3/8	9/16
230	29	33	36 7/8	1/4	1 1/4	1 1/2
235	24 3/4	29	31 1/2	1/2	1 1/2	1 5/8
240	21	22	25	1 1/16	2 1/8	2 7/8
245	16 3/8	19	21	1 7/8	3 3/8	3 5/8
250	11 1/4	13 3/4	16 1/2	3	4 5/8	5 1/8
255	8	11 1/2	12	4 3/4	7	8
260	5 5/8	8 1/4	10 1/2	7	9	10 1/4
265	3 7/8	6 1/2	8 3/4	10 1/4	12	9 1/2
270	2 9/16	4 5/8	7	14 1/2	14 1/2	12 1/2

Total call volume 424,844 Total call open int. 470,371
Total put volume 424,474 Total put open int. 778,801
The index: High 270.93; Low 257.32; Close 259.01, –4.47.

A box of the OEX reflecting the trading of January 23, 1987, a traumatic day for OEX traders.

disease of telephonitis (all lines clogged), and your nervous system was up to it, the best policy was to hunker down and do nothing. This kind of day, which occurred over two days in September (11 and 12) must be anticipated in our age of computer program trading. That means it can occur three or four times a year under present circumstances and more often if these circumstances change to favor such days.

The situation is unlike the so-called triple witching hour, which is a scheduled trauma four times a year when options expire—index options, equity options and options on the stock index futures (S&P 500). This trauma can be avoided as automatically as it occurs, simply by knowing when the triple witching hours occur and not scheduling any contracts that end at any of those times. In recent triple witching days not much has happened; some adjustments have been made and the days ended with normal trading. To be sure, the period immediately before has often been highly volatile, complicating avoidance strategies. Perhaps something will happen to ease program trading days, but it will take a supercomputer to effect such a cure.

When program trading days happen they are triggered upwards in buying programs keyed to the rise of the S&P 500 stock index futures sharply above the cash price and downwards when the 500 futures index drops below the cash price significantly. When either event occurs, the impact is as dramatic as a cannon shot. Volume increases sensationally on the upside or downside, depending on the direction of the index in relation to the cash price. If the market is going up, all the volume is on the buy side; if it is going down, everything is on the sell side. Once the programs run their course—and these episodes lash themselves out fairly quickly—the market reverts to its previous pattern, but in a much higher or lower channel. It is the stuff of 100 point days. It can happen at any time—at the beginning of a trading day or during the day. You cannot hedge against it unless you buy both a put and call (or X number of them) to cover any other transactions you have in the works, such as combinations, spreads or stock index futures. Because these are themselves partly hedging devices, the buying of puts and calls to balance possible losses in them is both ironic and precautionary. It is also difficult if not impossible.

Little advance warning of these violent episodes can be expected. They happen. But you *can* watch the S&P stock index futures (or have a broker who does), and when the futures' price begins to move without a tandem move in the cash price it is time for alarm. The least risky thing to do is to buy puts and calls. The best thing is to be out of such markets.

One should not buy puts and calls for hedging stocks in this situation. Stocks are mostly not affected by computer program trading.

Seductive Pose

The OEX stood at 259 on January 23, after a loss of about 4 1/2 points and a Dow drop of 44 points with a close of 2101. A four-week-away combination posed seductively in terms of rich premiums. A Feb 270 call at 2 9/16 and a 245 Feb put at 1 7/8 were hard to resist—selling them and bringing in almost 4 1/2 points ($450) per contract based on four weeks until expiration. Though we would have preferred to have a bigger cushion on the call side rather than the 14 points on the put side, because we believed the market was continuing to move upward, there was no 275 call on the board—it was posted the next day. So we sold the 25 point channel combination on a Friday.

The market dropped, then recovered, Monday, January 26, finishing up almost 6 points. The 270 call dropped slightly as did the 245 put. But the next day the 270 call went up to 3 1/4, the put dropped enough to compensate somewhat for the call's advance. The OEX index was up 3.72, the broader market was giving off signs of another major advance. Volume had been over 300 million shares on Friday, it dropped on Monday to about 130 million, spurting up again Tuesday to almost 200 million.

One cannot generalize about such volatility beyond noting that it causes premiums of the OEX and other options to enrich, tempting ever more players into the market. When volume rises in a bull market, the market usually goes up. Rising volume in a down market is a negative sign—the bull may be turning into a bear. This metamorphosis was nowhere in sight on the days in question. Also, any single day's signals are never the final judgment on the market overall. That is true of both positive and negative signals.

The presence of such volatility was a clear warning that combination selling was becoming too risky and that other strategies made more sense. Perhaps it was time to stand aside, giving the combinations a rest. But we didn't.

On January 27 the OEX gained another 3.72 points, as the Dow went up 43.17, again with close to 200 million shares. The OEX was now at 263, or 7 points away from the Feb 270 call. It was now at 3 1/4, while the 245 Feb put dropped to 15/16 from 1 7/8. Touchy but not too worrisome, except for the high volume.

January 28 continued the upward movement with the Dow gaining about 13 points. The Feb 270 call was now at 3 5/8, the 245 put at 3/4. The next day, January 29, the Dow dropped 3.38 points in an uneventful market day. Things were looking up, with the Feb 270 call dropping to 2 5/8, the 245 put up to 13/16.

January 30 produced more of the same, with volume dropping to just over 160 million shares and the OEX closing at 262.96, for a loss of .25. Now the 270 call was 2 1/8, the put 3/4.

Monday, February 2, produced an increase in volume and a Dow gain of about 21 points. The OEX was at 265.53, gaining 2.57. The 270 call was at 2 3/4, the 245 put was 7/16. The combination was still losing, but not by much. Because expiration was less than three weeks away we were reluctant to take the loss. On Tuesday it seemed that our hunch was vindicated. The Dow dropped about 11 points, and the OEX was off .89, with the 270 call at 2 1/4, the 245 put at 7/16. We continued to hang on, apprehensively, but not terribly alarmed, since we were ahead of the game on our bull spread and had bought calls in expectation of more upside momentum. February 4 sent the OEX up almost 3 1/2 points on a big volume day, moving the 270 call back up to 3 1/2, while dropping the put to 3/16. The next day was also a gainer, but not by much. The OEX gained 2 points, but the 270 call was now at an exposed 4 5/8. It was now in the money; we had a margin call as the OEX stood at 270.10. Our losses were estimable. We decided to check out the next morning's market and accept defeat if it continued to go against us.

The Dow didn't move much, despite heavy volume. We hung on and were rewarded with a drop in the OEX of 1.37 as it closed at 268.73, with the 270 call at 3 5/8, the 245 put at 1/8. We were still in the red but not by all that much. We decided to hold our position since Monday, February 9, was the next trading day and Mondays are usually down days. Our guess turned out to be a good one. The market dropped 10 points, the OEX dropped 1.70, and the 270 call fell to 1 13/16; the 245 put remained at 1/8. We were now about even.

We pushed our head above water Tuesday, February 10, with a drop in the Dow of 18.70 and an OEX close at 264.24, which was a drop of 2.79. Now the 270 call was 1 5/8, and the put was holding at 1/8. We had a solid profit. But we held on, perhaps foolishly.

February 11 continued the pattern of small changes in general market activity and indicators. The Dow closed up 14 points, the OEX 2.54, the Feb 270 call moved up to 2 1/4; the put remained at 1/16. We regretted not taking the profits the day before.

Our regrets were dispelled quickly February 12, when the Dow dropped slightly over 6 points, sending the OEX down almost 2 points! That put the Feb 270 call at 1 3/8—a sizeable gain for us—and the put remained at 1/16. Should we take profits? We decided to pig out and wait.

The old market saw about it being a place for bears and bulls but not for pigs came into operation the next day, Friday, February 13, a week from expiration. The Dow jumped a mere 17.57 points, but the OEX moved up almost 4. That sent the 270 call scurrying up to 2 5/16. Why such a jump in the OEX when the Dow gained only the equivalent of 2 1/4 OEX points? It happens.

We decided to wait until Monday and move according to early market returns. They were bullish, so we got out, but only with our skins intact. We had to buy back the calls at 3 for a loss, which was balanced out by a gain in the puts. Here's the way it ended. We lost 7/16 on the calls but gained 1 13/16 on

This shows the Dow Jones Transportation Average moving from 800 to 900 from December 30, 1986, to January 23, 1987, more or less synchronized with the industrials.

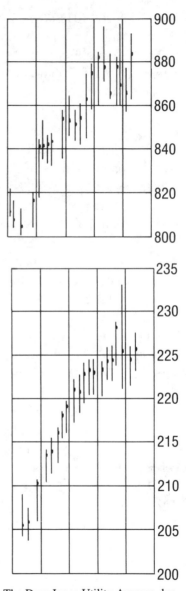

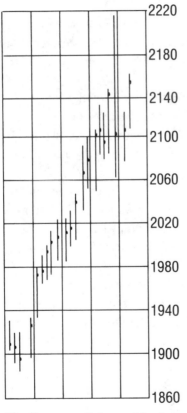

The Dow moved in roughly three weeks from about 1900 to 2215, then back to 2060 in a single day. The movement shows the risk in combination selling. This happened in January 1987.

The Dow Jones Utility Average during the same period as the above, conforming to the overall Dow movement.

the puts, for a gain of 1 3/8. We had ten contracts. Multiplying 1 3/8 times 10 gave us a profit of $1,375 on a margin investment of about $10,000 originally, plus about $2,500 on a margin call. (Margin money is put into an interest-bearing account.) Because the environment was hostile—the market was going up almost continuously, with many wild swings during the day that aroused anxiety if nothing else—we had to be pleased to make profits, even though reduced. The time period was just under four weeks. In our total strategy, which also involved bull spreads and the buying of calls as well as the S&P 500 stock index futures, our total earnings were much higher.

New Strategy

The market was making us wary about combinations. We watched with a fishy eye until Monday, February 23, when we decided to do another combination, using an even more cautious strategy that consisted of a wider channel. (There are only two basic cautionary strategies: widen the channel, shorten the time.)

We were looking at a 272.21 OEX index on a day when the market dropped about 19 Dow points. Yet we believed that the market would be going higher, based on our analysis and that of others. What we saw was a market that hadn't gone down much since it dropped 200 points in September 1986, mostly in two days, the eleventh and twelfth. Resistance to drop is an invariable sign of a bull market, despite the age of this market whose bullishness commenced in August 1982. More important, there were no signs of larger events that could make the market lose its character. Corporate profits were strong, the economy, though sluggish, was moving along on an even keel, unemployment was moderate, and no events overseas were threatening. So, if we were convinced that the market was going higher, why did we rush into another combination, which is profitable only when the market hems and haws?

We interpreted the history of our last combination to be a sign that you could come out ahead even in a relentlessly moving market, if events worked in your favor. These events consisted primarily of the discovery that the huge volatilities, so dangerous to combination playing, tended to even themselves out, so that the general market was largely untouched. The stunning changes on September 11 and 12, and on January 23, were not identical in this respect. The September 11 drop from 1870 to 1780 (approximately) and the drop from 1800 to about 1735 the next day, ended a decline. The market then gathered strength, moving up and down from September 12 to October 10, but girding for the huge drive upward. The shocking events of January 23, in which the market moved between 2060 and 2220 (approximately) all in one day, but settled around 2100, was an ordinary day if you look at a chart. The day before the market had closed around 2140, but on the big day of January 23 it closed around 2100, for a drop of about 40 points (approximate numbers). But a 40-point drop is common nowadays, and on the next day the market resumed its upward march, with a period between February 5 and 13 when it was moving back and forth with volatility. But if you draw a trend line from January 2 through March 20, when there was another big drop, you will see that it is a straight up progression. In other words, the basics were untouched by the events of January 23.

A New Tack

Thus with the OEX at 272.21 we decided to change tactics, allowing for enormously more volatile days, using a wider channel between the upper call and the lower put. We sold Apr 290s at 2 3/4 and 250 Apr puts at 1 7/16, for a total of 4 3/16, or about $418. Ten contracts brought in about $4,180, minus commissions, with about $10,000 margin. We were also using bull spreads and buying OEX calls and the S&P 500 sporadically. So we resorted to a 40 point spread and, roughly, a seven-week expiration. This was altogether a new tack for us. Forty OEX points figure out to a Dow move of 280 points, or 140 up and 140 down. We were betting that such moves would not occur in the next seven weeks.

Through March 3 our bet looked safe indeed. On March 4 the OEX jumped up almost 5 points to 278.63, accompanying a Dow move up of 31 points. That meant our upper limit of 290 was only about 12 OEX points or 84 Dow points away. Comforting though was that the 250 Apr puts had declined to 1/2 from 1 7/16 as the 290 call went from 2 3/4 to 3 1/8.

March 5 brought an advance of the OEX to 280.41 as the Dow moved up 19 points—an OEX gain of 1.78 points. Volume was building with over 205 million shares changing hands on the NYSE.

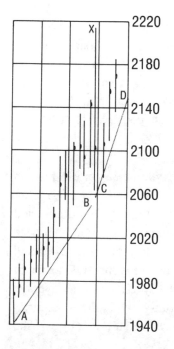

Despite the huge volatilities at X (January 23, 1987), if you draw a trendline from A to B and C to D, it is fairly obvious that the basic thrust of the market was not changed by the drama of the day's events.

A week later, March 10, the OEX stood at 280.93, the 290 Apr call was at 2 13/16, the 250 put at 5/16. Despite large intraday moves on March 9 and 10, the combination was okay.

Six days later the OEX was around 277. On March 17 it jumped almost 5 points, to 282.66. The Apr 290 call was at 3, the 250 put at 1/8.

The OEX was creeping up the next few days until March 20, when it jumped 4.47 points to 288.22, perilously close to margin call territory and losses. The 290 call was at 4 1/4. We decided to abandon the combination if the market went against us the next morning, which was a Monday, March 23.

When the market opened on fairly large volume, trading down at first, but soon changing direction upward, we left the trade. We emerged from it at 4 ($400). The profit on the put side was $1,400; the loss on the call side was $1,250. We had sold it for a total of about 4 3/16, so we left with enough money to cover the commissions. We left with our skin.

The Dow was now closing in on the 2400 mark. We watched the action, uncertain of our next combination move.

Somewhat gun-shy over the failure of the most conservative tactic we had yet employed—a channel of 40 points, or double the earlier size—we were not reassured at the market leap above 2400 intraday, March 27. On the same day the OEX traded in a 6-point range. We decided to keep our powder dry for the nonce.

On April 3 the market had a big volume day of 215 million shares and a trading range between 2320 and 2390. We were delighted not to be caught in it, as program traders dominated the play. We were disturbed at the volatility and uncertainty of market direction. It turned out to be straight up to 2400 and straight down to—we knew not where. We were convinced that the market was in a correction, especially as the utilities average had been dropping since early February, while the transportation average had been going sideways, though it followed the general direction of the big moves in the industrial average. These divergences, as they are called, sometimes alert market technicians to a change in market direction. We didn't want to ignore them. The basic strategy at this point was the buying of OEX puts and, for the boldest spirits, the selling of the S&P 500 stock index futures, about which we'll talk more later.

Monday, April 6, was not the usual blue Monday. A small rally carried up 15 points on the Dow and the OEX moved up 2 points to 293.63. Nothing in these and other indicators made us jump up and down—or into the market. The next day the Dow dropped 44.60, and on declining volume it rose 11.22 the following day, April 8. It began to look like combination territory—trendless.

A drop of 33 Dow points on April 9, with a drop of 4 points in the OEX, lent mild confirmation, with no bells ringing yet. April 10 continued the general pattern, but intraday the market was extremely volatile, jumping around more than 50 points on declining but essentially trendless volume. The volatility frightened us away, luckily enough, as the market dropped almost 52 points the following Monday, April 13. Now we worried that we had missed a bear spread and the sale of the stock index futures contract. Both would have been winners. The market again was highly volatile and refused to go below 2200, which we took to be a resistance point, perhaps even a temporary bottom, since all three Dow components struck way down and bounced way up. Given the volatility— the big intraday swings—we decided to try both a combination and a bull spread, though we were holding a May bull spread (no law says you can't have more than one at a time, if your courage-caution index is favorable).

Why use both these somewhat contradictory tactics, since a bull spread requires a trending up market whereas a combination needs a trendless, listless market or one that doesn't stray too far from a central Dow trading point? The combination we sought would have a wide margin of safety, since we were looking for a close-in expiration date and a 30 point or greater channel between the put and the call, to allow for the possibility of a continuation of the big swings that characterized so much of recent trading.

The bull spread would take advantage of the wide swings, since we had seen that some 45–50 point daily moves would allow us to make almost the complete profit possible in such a trade.

In effect, we were looking for a situation in which we would have our cake and eat it too.

On Tuesday, April 14, when the market opened on a downward thrust, in continuation of the day before, when it had dropped 52 points, the market began to firm and return from its bottom in the afternoon, after plunging to the 2215 area. On a chart it looked like a triple bottom formation, based on roughly similar low points March 13 and March 27. Triple bottoms are not magic; they guarantee nothing and they may well withhold everything. They are as much mystery as revelation, but they are something. They do indicate levels that provoke major institutional support or selling—computer programs based on much previous buying and selling.

With the OEX index at about 275 on Tuesday, April 14, a May 295 call had a premium of 2 7/8, a 260 May put a premium of 1 1/2. This represented a highly cautious channel of 35 points, yet profitable enough at 4 3/8 per contract. We sold five contracts that brought in almost $2,200 (4 3/8 times 5 equals 2188). The 35-point channel meant that the market had to move 245 points—half up, half down—before either side of the combination would be imperilled. The margin requirement, increasing as the market had been moving up, would come to around $10,000 for the five contracts.

The market splashed up 30 points the next day, April 15, but the OEX went up 5, instead of the expected 4 plus. That cut

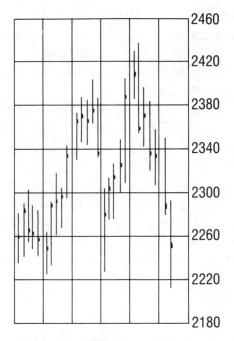

A triple bottom formation on March 13, 27, and April 14. These mysterious formations sometimes indicate the start of another big move upwards—but not always.

a swath through our comfortable channel on the very first day, which was hardly a reassuring development. In dollars and cents it hardly mattered; the combination was about the same.

Thursday, April 16, was kinder. The market dropped about 7 points. The combination changed, with the call gaining bafflingly, the put declining graciously. We remained about even.

The next week was uneventful, but on Friday, April 24, the market dropped more than 45 points. This was refreshing indeed for the pallid combination; it suddenly turned the color of green. Now the call eroded from 2 7/8 to 1 5/8, the put from 1 1/2 to 1 1/8, too early to cash in but not to cheer up a bit.

Little action ensued until Thursday, April 30, when the Dow closed up 32 points, the OEX up 3.69. Our combination looked like this: the 295 call was 1 3/4, and the 260 put was 5/16, compared to the original numbers of 2 7/8 and 1 1/2. With the OEX index now at 283.41, we were up—from 275—almost 8 1/2 points. We were, however, a long way from the 295 upper limit.

May Day brought no revolutionary developments, only calm. Tuesday, May 5, sent a rocket into the air; the Dow jumped 52 points, the OEX 6.64. The index now stood at 291.25, too close for comfort to the 295 call, which now expanded back to 2 5/8. Should we cash in our chips and get out at a tiny profit? We had expected a market rise; the triple bottom argued such a turn. We were, as always, uncertain of market breadth and force. Various indicators were not unanimous, and until they are we don't go whole hog. Meanwhile, our bull spread was working so well that we were being tempted into buying calls as added reinforcement. Our general position was well in the profit column, thanks to the bull spread.

Thursday, May 7, six trading days from expiration and thus complete triumph for our combination, saw the market drop, blissfully for us. The 295 call was smiling at us with a 1 3/4 price tag on its beatific face, the put even saintlier at 1/16. The OEX index was at 290 or 5 points from the disaster area. We resolved to hang in, despite the clear profit and the knowledge that a single huge eruption up would spell not relief but its aspirin opposite. We were ahead by 2 5/8, or about $1,300 over a period of a little more than three weeks. Not bad, not great, but comforting in an age of congressional investigations, AIDS headlines and other disasters.

More from inertia than conviction, we resisted taking the $1,300. Friday was its own reward; the market dropped a bit, our 295 collapsed like a balloon, down to 1 3/16; the index subsided to 288.58. Since most Mondays are blue for bulls, we made no plans to cash in Monday, May 11. A good thing; the

Dow dropped 15 points, our 295 call sank to 11/16 and the put remained at 1/16. So we were at 12/16, i.e., 3/4 of a point from Platonic perfection. Again, rashly, we decided to go for broke, with the OEX at a comfortable 286.51, 8 1/2 points below the thin red line of 295. We didn't feel much at risk.

Tuesday, May 12, saw volume drop off, reassuringly, but the Dow closed up 15.30, the OEX up almost 3. The 295 call was at 7/8, the put remained at 1/16. Wednesday was similar, with the Dow moving up 7, the OEX about 1; the 295 call was at 3/4, the put at 1/16. The OEX index was at 290.44, less than 5 points from the red line of 295.

Again we did nothing, as much from inertia as from conviction. The next two days went by without much volume or volatility, and most of the intraday changes were on the down or favorable side. We pocketed the entire swag of $2,180, minus commissions, in about a month.

If you ask why this combination succeeded completely and the others ran a gamut of performance, though mostly good, the first answer is a shrug—who knows? Still, the triple bottom in the Dow was a fairly good indication that the market wasn't going down. But how high was up? The triple bottom offered more reassurance for the bull spread, which also won. The buying of calls, and for the bold the S&P 500 index contract, were part of a spectrum of benefits to be generated by an upward moving market. But the combination succeeded in spite of the upward move. The final answer comes to our choice of channel and time—the 35 points were a safe haven, secure from the upward move, even though things got risky for a few days, and the shortness of time finally came to the rescue, like the cavalry from Fort Sill in the old Western movies.

Three Years Later

On December 13, 1989, we put on a combination spread; we sold five Feb 340 calls for 5 3/4, and five Feb 310 puts for 3, with the OEX at 331. That is a channel of 30 points with 21 points between the OEX and the put side and 9 points on the call side. Why the bearish bias? In volatile markets investors and speculators must also be volatile.

The income from the sale was $4,375 (5 3/4 from the calls equals $2,875 and 3 points from the puts, also times five contracts, equals $1,500). Now we wait for the market to do nothing.

For the next few days the market obliged. It hemmed and hawed inconclusively. A drop of 6 OEX points on December 18 caught our attention, but we were well cushioned for it—our puts were the 310s and the OEX was now at 323, a safe distance.

Two weeks later the combination looked like this: the 340 calls, sold for 5 3/8, were now at 3 4/8; the 310 puts, sold for 3 were 3. So we had a profit of about 2 points or $1,000. We held on.

On Tuesday, January 2, the market shot up and the OEX with it, closing at 336, dangerously close to our 340 calls. The 340 calls, sold for 5 3/4, were now at 5 1/2. The 310 puts, sold for 3, were at 2 1/8. We were about even, and margin outlays of $25,000 didn't seem to justify three weeks or so of trading back and forth.

The market receded over the next several trading days. On January 5 the OEX was at 330. Our Feb 340 calls, sold for 5 3/4, were now back to 3 1/2 (they had jumped up). The Feb 310 puts, sold for 3, were a 3 1/8. We regretted not taking the $1,000.

The market rested over the next several days, but on January 12 there was a big drop and the OEX went down to 319, 9 points above our 310 puts. Here's what the scoreboard said: the 340 calls, sold for 5 3/4, were now 1 1/16, the 310 puts, sold for 3, were a 6 1/8. We were 3 1/8 points in the red on the put side but 4 1/16 points on right side in the calls.

On January 17 the OEX dropped 3 points, closing at 317. Our 340 calls were at 9/16, but the 310 puts were at 5 3/8. Sad.

On January 19 the Dow turned up and the OEX was as high as 320. The 310 puts were at 3 1/2, the 340 calls were at 2. We had a deficit of 1/2 point or $250 on the puts; we were 3 3/4 points on the call side in the black —they were down to 1/16. Our profit was 3 points, or a total of $1,500 minus commissions. Not very good for the amount of margin money required, and the time involved —about five weeks, some of them worrisome.

The day after we ended the combination the market took its stunning 77 point drop. Had we maintained our position we would have lost several points. But we did own puts on that day, and other options—spreads that were profitable.

On January 24, we tried another combination. With the OEX at 310, we sold five Feb 325 calls for 1 1/2 and five Feb 295 puts for 2 5/8, taking a total of $2,065 along for the ride. Too often it can be no more than that. Less than a month remained; we gambled that no more crisis days would intervene.

By February 5 the market had cooperated. The 325 calls went from 1 1/2 to 5/16 so we had over a point there (times five contracts). The 295 puts went from 2 5/8 to 1 1/4 so we had over 5 points there. Thus a profit of over $1,000 in the space of about two weeks. We held on.

The market noodled around for the next several days, doing exactly what we desired—nothing. The 325 calls remained at 5/16; the 295 puts were at 7/16. The sky had brightened.

On Monday, February 12, the OEX dropped almost 3 points. Our 325 calls, sold for 1 1/2, were now 1/16; the 295 puts, sold for 2 5/8, were 9/16. Good show.

Should we exit this trade? The OEX was at 310, our puts at 295 seemed secure, as did our calls at 325. What did we have to lose by holding out? (The answer is sleep; but we did.)

On Monday, February 12, the OEX lost 3 points, finishing at 309. The market continued to rock back and forth, according to our best scenario. Our options went out on expiration day, February 15, giving us a total of over $2,000, in a period of about four weeks.

I conclude that combination selling, while much more expensive than it was several years ago when I addressed it in greater detail, remains potentially profitable, given appropriate hedging tactics along with it. But with the high margin costs, that vary from as low as $20,000 to as much as $100,000, far fewer speculators rally round its flag.

Strategy Four:
Buying Puts and Calls

First Principles

The first thing to notice about OEX calls (and all others) is that they often cost more than puts. Nobody knows exactly why, but speculation has it that people prefer to think optimistically about the economy and the market. The up direction seems a more optimistic goal than down since that is unequivocally true about stocks and their direction. Options commenced as surrogates for stocks. This relationship, though now vestigial because of all the new roles played by options, remains psychologically true at least. It translates into the often higher valuation placed on calls, even though for our purposes direction is a neutral feature of the option landscape. We conform to what the market does when we sell combinations and employ spreads, though the latter do involve market timing. When we buy calls we attempt to profit by what is in effect a guess about direction. Our total strategy in buying calls is based upon certain hard principles of selection, which have very little or nothing to do with guesswork.

Eliminating Guesswork

A glance at an OEX table shows that on the day when the OEX closed at 230 (it was actually 230.03), the nearest call was a 235 at 1/16, the nearest put was a 225 also at 1/16. As we have just solemnly declared that calls are more expensive than puts, usually, and have now produced evidence that they are identical in price—the put and the call are equally distant from the closing price of the OEX and, hence, should, if the theory is correct, reflect this with a higher price for the call—have made us out to be a liar. But we picked the closing day of the OEX cycle, which happened to be the third Friday in November, November 21, 1986. Because both the 225 put and the 235 call were out-of-the-money, lacking intrinsic or real value, and were on the expiration day of the cycle, having exhausted all time value, they were now on their last legs, so to speak. A 1/16 is the least possible amount of time or other value. Moreover, it isn't always true that calls are more expensive than puts. Enter psychology. When market players think the market is going down they bid up the value of puts. There are other reasons why it sometimes happens that put premiums get larger than calls.

Chicago Board 11/20/86

S&P 100 INDEX

Strike	Calls—Last			Puts—Last		
Price	Nov	Dec	Jan	Nov	Dec	Jan
205	23¼	....	22½	1/16	⅛	7/16
210	16¾	....	16¾	1/16	5/16	¾
215	15	13⅝	13⅝	1/16	9/16	1 5/16
220	10	11¼	11¾	1/16	1¼	2⅜
225	5	7⅛	8⅛	1/16	2½	3⅞
230	15/16	4⅛	5⅜	1 1/16	4⅜	6¾
235	1/16	1 15/16	3⅜	5¼	8½	9
240	....	¾	2	13½	12½	12½
245	....	¼	15/16	15⅞	17⅞	....
250	....	1/16	....	23¾	....	....

Total call volume 252,702 Total call open int. 646,836
Total put volume 222,626 Total put open int. 858,302
The index: High 230.04; Low 225.43; Close 230.03, +4.61.

The OEX Index showing identical 1/16 prices for puts and calls nearest the closing index price. This is not the usual state of affairs—calls cost more than puts for the most part.

Best Time to Buy

The best single use of buying OEX options occurs in those cases where the market goes against you, and it seems you are about to lose a lot of money, or at any rate the maximum possible amount. In these situations, assuming that you are on top of them, or have an alert broker who is authorized to trade for you, the buying of OEX options resembles the cavalry coming to the rescue in the old Western movies. It can do amazing things.

To refresh your memory (and ours): we were involved in a combination that we sold August 20, 1986, based on an OEX index of about 230, with a call at 245, a put at 220. With the channel between the call and the index larger than the one we picked for the put and index (15 versus 10 points), we betrayed our bullish bias. We thought the market was going up. It did, for the next several weeks. Our combination became profitable around September 9, and we took profits. But many people would have been tempted to stay on, flushed with success, thinking they could gain 100 percent of potential profits. Then came September 11, and the 86 point collapse in the Dow. Those remaining in the market were advised to take five steps: (1) buy back the losing puts, (2) put on a bear spread, (3) wait for the dust to settle—for market calm—and resell more puts so as to reestablish the combo, (4) use the S&P 500 stock index futures, and (5) buy as many OEX put options as you could afford, doing it around 9:30 in the morning. Your nose had to be to the wheel to take such advice. Your emotions had to be under control in circumstances in which everything seemed to be coming apart.

In crisis situations buying options becomes a saving grace, if you are level-headed enough to recognize a crisis and able enough to avoid psychological paralysis.

Crisis can arise any time, but we define it to mean a single day's spurt, up or down when the market goes against your positions, in combinations or spreads. Can you prepare for such a situation?

Yes, with the combination above, and many similar ones, which we made profitable, several days before September 11, but that many others would have held through the two big down days, September 11 and 12. All you had to do was to buy a put-call combination on the day you decided *not* to sell and hold on in hopes of making your 100 percent profit from expiration (third Friday, September 1986).

Whenever you feel that greed has overcome reason in the trading of combinations and spreads (a feeling you must cultivate along with other endearing emotions), there is a simple, fairly inexpensive way out of the dilemma. Early in September the market was showing signs of danger ahead, lurching back and forth through the first seven trading days. Faced with such a market, but determined to hold positions in spreads and combinations, you should always buy a put-call combination.

In the dilemma we're talking about, you could have bought an OEX 235 Sep put and 240 call on September 5, with the OEX index at 236.41, for a total of $450 per contract. On September 12, after the fall, each contract would have ballooned to $1,600, for a gain of 250 percent in a week.

Why the put-call combination when elsewhere we talk about buying only the put side? Indeed we do, but that is the tactic to be pursued on the calamity day when it is too late to take precautionary measures, like the combination offers. On September 11 and 12 no precautions were available, only the five crisis strategies we have described. But a week earlier the buying of a put-call combination as a hedge against existing spreads and combinations would have been an excellent additional profit-making strategy, as well as an inspired precautionary move. The call side of such a combination would have been wasted, but it may be considered an investment. You can't win everything all the time.

Wouldn't it do just as well to buy combinations in every unstable market situation? Yes, that is an excellent, automatic approach to the OEX, and it works more often than not, but overall its profitability is less than the course we prescribe. The trick to making large profits, of course, is to time the market correctly, and even the best gurus have been known to fail, including us, and we lay no claim to being the best.

If you want to concentrate on buying combinations to the exclusion of other activities, you can begin by using the market indicators we set out fully in the chapter on the S&P 500 futures index, which have served us well in market timing.

Tracking the Trades

The probabilities of guessing market direction with enough accuracy to win at buying options are always less than 25 percent. Buying option combinations, in conjunction with selling combinations and spreading options, is a form of insurance and sometimes a profit generator. If you catch a long trend it can turn into a big money maker. Meanwhile, you can expect a lot of small losses. The trick is to keep them that way.

As we explain elsewhere, the trading we're recommending in this chapter is defensive in an environment that screams for effective defensive strategy. Again we emphasize that options money should never take precedence over any of the basic forms of investing, which are: blue chip stocks, bonds, U.S. Government paper, real estate, and precious metals. Coins and collectibles belong in here somewhere, but they require highly specialized expertise.

Around the middle of 1986 the market was unusually volatile and frightening to old line investors. The Dow was gyrating between about 1940 and 1740 within remarkably short periods of time. In the past, when the Dow was below 1,000, it could take months to move 100 points, but in July 1986, the market dropped from 1880 to about 1830 on July 5 and down to 1780 the next day. We have already noted the swing down from 1870 to 1735 on September 11 and 12. Then came January 23, 1987, and its gyrations, described elsewhere. Month after month this pattern of high volatility persisted, making options play risky but not impossible, as we've already seen. Such huge movements, up and down, attract option players like moths to the flame, often with similar results. A move in the OEX of 3 points, which is common, means $300 profit or loss, if you have the right strike price. If you own ten contracts the dollars turn into $3,000 in a single day.

The OEX has moved as much as 14 points in a single day, or $1,400 per contract. On September 11, 1986, when the market dropped 85 points, an OEX put, if bought in-the-money, had a potential of moving 12 points (which it did), and all you had to do was catch a half or a third of the move to profit handsomely. This requires the closest possible attention to markets, which most people may not be willing to undertake.

But on that day the market showed its hand immediately. Within minutes of the opening bell the Dow spurted down, and by 9:30 all the puts were ringing their own bells. At this point, a bona fide options player would have bought puts either at-the-money or in-the-money, so as to guarantee movement by the puts in tandem with the market. (Buying out-of-the-money options means that the market has to catch up with them before it sweeps them along.) Around 9:30 it was still possible to buy a put for around 4 or 5 (if you could get through to your broker) that would be worth 14 or 15 by day's end, and far more than that had you held it through the next day's trading. But that's a Johnny-on-the-spot operation, too hectic for most people to contemplate. A market follower would have been pondering a bear spread on September 5 or 6, or about that time, sufficiently before September 11 to do something about it. The tandem operation should include the buying of puts, and in an extremely volatile market like this one, the buying of a put and call combination. The call would have been a total loss at the time (but not if you held it to expiration date), whereas the put was a potential gold mine.

Again, remember the signals for these actions. The market had been moving from around 1700 to around 2000, in wide sweeps that carried it irresistibly up. On the eruption from 1720 to 1930, which led to the September 11 and 12 drop, volume also built up explosively, though not in a straight line up. It all looked extremely bullish. But meanwhile, the advance/decline line (number of stocks going up versus going down) was not expanding, and in view of the accumulating upward momentum in the market that had been going on for months, with about four or five minor corrections, market timers were talking correction. It made common sense as well, since you had merely to glance at the previous six or seven months of market action to see that a pattern had evolved. It consisted of widening swings up and down, always with higher highs, which market technicians all agree means a higher market with ever increasing dangers of corrections. But the corrections had been coming along in small doses, so the big one that occurred between September 5 and 12 was almost totally expected.

We are talking now about the Dow which was going its own sweet way, broadly, since about the end of May 1986, while the transportation average was moving almost opposite to the industrials, and the utilities were going up but not correcting or making wide swings with the industrials. So something had to give in the fateful week of September 5 thru 12.

Why did something have to give? Because these indexes are not abstractions. They represent what major fund managers believe about the economy. If major divergences occur between components of the Dow, causing airlines, trains, trucks and ships to go one way while industrials go another and utilities yet another, indicating schisms of belief in the economy, the overall market will reflect these divisions. Markets function on agreements not disputes, as traders sign and seal their positions. When wide disagreements arise, such as happened in the period above, there will often be violent resolutions, as in other fields of human behavior.

What Were the Options?

In these divergent situations, when major market players disagree—for in effect that is what is going on—it behooves the rest of us to run for cover, or at least get out of the way.

In the situation above, the buying of a put-call combination was certainly far less risky than doing nothing, if you were in the market and played options at all. In this combination you look for immediate, dramatic gains on one side with loss on the other. The trick is to take the gains and sweat out the loss on the assumption that reaction to violent moves in one way will take the market to the other way and salvage the losing position. It does not happen every time but often enough to warrant playing as if it does. In the present instance it did. If you bought a put-call combination far enough out you would have won on both sides. The put was profitable immediately, the call turned that way in November.

The market went into low gear after the drama of September 11 and 12, but that was the Dow, the thirty industrials. This was not so with the twenty transportation stocks. They moved up sharply, from a low of 720 to 800 (they, of course, have their own average, as do the utilities). One must notice all three components when doing anything with the stock market and options. A glance at the charts of the three averages shows that they were not marching in harmony, as traditional theory expects in a normal bull market, and as common sense argues in agreement. The industrials were looping up and down, in ever-widening swings while making higher highs and higher lows in the process. The transportation average, by contrast, was working its way down to a bottom on August 1, 1986, from which it launched a big move up. The utilities were moving almost opposite to the transportation average, moving on a long sweep upward until they dropped sharply in September, then built another base.

These divergences indicate a market that reflects an uncertain economy, according to some observers. In theory, the general market should have gone nowhere at the time. But it did. The Dow went from around 1700 to almost 2000. As we know, the swings were wide enough and lengthy enough in time to allow our combinations to bear fruit but not so spaced out in time as to prevent bull and bear spreads from working— you want them to work quickly, though often they are reluctant to do so. So why is it necessary to buy spreads or individual puts and calls? For those events that don't allow sufficient time for the other strategies to work. Also, for hedging.

Around the last week in September 1986, the three components of the Dow averages began finally to move together. The industrials moved from 1740 to 1800, the transportations from 760 to 800 and the utilities from around 200 to 205. Volume was also building. All the signs for a bull spread and the buying of OEX calls were present. But technical signals like these are not foolproof; the market, as if to remind us, took a downturn the next few days. It also lost the consensus it had effected between the three Dow components, with utilities going against the transportation and industrial averages. Market technicians get wary at these differences.

On October 1 matters seemed again to augur well for a general market upturn. At that point we decided that buying OEX calls was a good thing, along with being in a bull spread—which we were. We bought the Oct 220s at 4 7/8, with the market at 1782.90 and the OEX index at 221.59. It was an in-the-money option with an expiration date three weeks away. We've stressed before that when you buy options, as opposed to selling them, you buy them in-the-money. They cost more, but they pay more when they pay.

October 2 saw the Dow lose a couple of points with the OEX gaining a trifle. The Oct 220s, bought at 4 7/8, were at 5 3/8, for a gain of $50.

By October 13 it was clear we had made a mistake. The Dow had waffled; it refused to move up, hemming and hawing around the 1840 area. Our call was in the red by several hundred dollars, which isn't much by investment or speculative standards. A week away from expiration, we saw more red. We decided to go for broke. Wednesday, October 15, saw the Dow jump 31 1/2 points, the OEX move up 4, and our 220s move to 6. We breathed a sigh of small profit (small sigh) and walked away in sadness. We gained 1 1/8 points on each of the five options we bought, thus making about $500.

No reason presented itself to get us involved in buying options for the next few days, though the Dow took a 26 point jump October 30, and any move of 30 points means that the OEX will move 4 or 5 points, so that five contracts will balloon up to $2,500 for the day. But it isn't all that easy to catch such moves. It is not like fishing in a barrel.

We were in a bull spread on November 3 when the question of buying calls arose. Again we consulted the three Dow averages, finding the industrials continuing their rise, the transportations and utilities continuing theirs in tandem. We took the plunge. November 3 saw the OEX at 232, the November 230s at 3 3/4. We bought five of them, priced at $1,875, plus commissions.

The trouble with in-the-money options is that they are sensitive reeds; they are not for the faint of heart. Every fluctuation of the market moves them, unlike out-of-the-money options, which bow less to the winds of change. Nervous types should never buy in-the-money options (or sell them).

On November 13 the market dipped 31 1/2 points, our calls dropping to less than 1 point. So we faced an almost total loss of our roughly $2,000. We decided to go for broke, come what may, since we were far ahead of the options game and a loss of $2,000 didn't seem all that terrible. (It was, however, a hefty percentage of the money we allot to playing options, which isn't much since our chief activity is in blue chip stocks and others.)

Friday, November 14, a week from expiration, saw the Dow move up 11 points, the OEX up 1.60 and the Nov 230s up to 1 7/8, a far cry from the original cost of 3 3/4, but enough of a move to cause a faint stirring of hope. We held on.

The market went into its usual Monday torpor on November 17, losing 13 points, dropping the Nov 230s to 1 1/4. The temptation was strong to cut our losses and run. But we waited. Patience is an elderly virtue that pays off in blue chip stocks held over the years. Would it work in the heated environment of OEX options where every minute brings a change of signal and direction?

Tuesday brought the worst disaster of all, a market drop of 43 points, an OEX drop of over 5, and the shredding of our Nov 230s. They were now at 3/16. Ouch! Now there was no reason to sell but every reason to hold to the bitter end. On Wednesday the OEX moved up 1.61 points, the Nov 230s held bitterly at 3/16. We turned a deaf eye. Thursday saw a slight rebound, with the Nov 230s up to 15/16. The market itself had jumped over 34 points and the OEX was up 2.40, which was disappointing but true. The final day, Friday, November 21 (expiration) saw the condemned option eat a hearty meal. The market, on strong volume, moved up fairly rapidly and so did the OEX. The Nov 230s recovered magnificently to 3 5/8, which means that we wound up at a virtual tie.

There is a weak moral in all this trading back and forth. Don't panic, even when it seems the only sensible thing to do. No matter how badly you are treated by the market today, it doesn't follow that the same thing will happen tomorrow. In affairs of this sort, the market differs from reality, where a beating today may well be followed by a worse one tomorrow. It's a question of environment; in a bull market the environment is always potentially favorable.

A relieved weekend followed, uncluttered with worry over the expiration of calls. Monday saw the market move cautiously up and down, finishing up 12 1/2 points and in effect continuing the fairly robust advance of the November 12 to 21 period. This advance began to run out of steam over the next few days, lending strength to our combination that was in place. However, we missed a golden opportunity to buy calls when the market jumped 43 points on December 2. A bull spread on this day

A

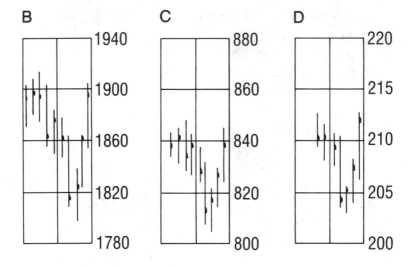

Chicago Board   11/21/86

S&P 100 INDEX

Strike Price	Calls—Last Nov	Dec	Jan	Puts—Last Nov	Dec	Jan
205	25⅞	....	26¼	....	¹⁄₁₆	⅜
210	20⅜	23½	20½	....	³⁄₁₆	⁹⁄₁₆
215	18¾	18	17	¹⁄₁₆	⁷⁄₁₆	1¹⁄₁₆
220	13⅝	13⅝	14¾	¹⁄₁₆	¹⁵⁄₁₆	1⅞
225	8⅝	9	10¼	¹⁄₁₆	1¾	3⅛
230	3⅝	5	7	¹⁄₁₆	3⅜	5
235	¹⁄₁₆	2⁹⁄₁₆	4⅛	1⁵⁄₁₆	5¾	7½
240	¹⁄₁₆	⅞	2⅜	6½	9⅞	10¼
245	....	⅜	1³⁄₁₆	....	12½	....
250	....	¹⁄₁₆	....	18½	....	....

Total call volume 448,443   Total call open int. 633,235
Total put volume 257,557   Total put open int. 881,766
The index: High 234.14; Low 229.66; Close 233.68, +3.65.

B

1940
1900
1860
1820
1780

C

880
860
840
820
800

D

220
215
210
205
200

The OEX Index shows the recovery that made our spread respectable (but not profitable). The market signals shown by the inserts make it clear that we had every reason to expect a very strong recovery in the shortest possible time, which is exactly what we were counting on and is the only situation that makes our behavior rational. Thus the B chart shows how the industrials dropped sharply for about a week, and then reversed and commenced a powerful upward spurt.

The C chart shows that the transportation stocks were in agreement with the industrials.

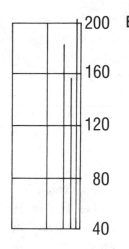

200   E

160

The D chart shows that the utilities were equally bullish. These tandem moves—extremely desirable in any hoped-for upward move were much strengthened by the E chart (volume) which leaped up to 200 million shares from 160, which is not exactly peanuts.

120

80

40

would have paid off handsomely, too, as the OEX closed up 5 points, which is sometimes enough to double your money in a single day. Fortunately for us, we had such a spread.

For a week the industrials were sleeping. A 16 point advance December 10 was the only notable change, and in a market flirting with 2000, such an advance is a minor percentage blip.

In the next period, leading to Christmas, the market was working hard for our combinations. There was no traditional Christmas rally; we saw no reason to buy options.

The Dow averages spent the next few days trading at low volume, with the industrials moving sideways, the transportation stocks declining, the utilities showing a slight downward bias.

A mighty gathering of forces arose in the new year. Friday, just after New Year's eve, the Dow was up 31.36, the OEX up 5 points, sustaining loosely the ratio of 1 OEX point for every 7 Dow points. When the OEX fails to deliver on this ratio it means that some of the bellwether stocks in the index are not doing their duty—the blue chip brigade is not moving in lockstep, which is bearish, not bullish, even when the Dow averages go up. Even so, with all three Dow components suddenly seeing the same light, beginning January 2, and moving together, and with bells ringing throughout the market as they had not been doing recently, we decided to wait a day or so for more confirmation. We did, however, enter a bull spread, which is the more conservative way to play a burgeoning, unconfirmed upward move. If there is a psychological component to every market move, the psychology of such a moment as we faced is complex and difficult to master. The market, in the first week of the new year (1987) was going up day after day, and we were doing a bull spread, which is a coward's way to play an upwardly trending market. The imaginative (i.e. risky) way is to buy options as well as the S&P 500 index futures, a heavy artillery vehicle we wheel out only on those rare occasions when we think we have the message from on high—BUY. But don't these two vehicles overlap—the buying of calls and 500 futures? Profits don't overlap; they are adders (harmless snakes that resemble vipers; if you don't catch them you feel stung).

What sold us finally was the daily increase in volume of the OEX; it was a crescendo worthy of Tchaikovsky. We took the plunge.

The Plunge

On Tuesday, January 6, we bought 3 OEX calls, with the index at 240.89. These were the Feb 240s, in-the-money, for 5 5/8. We spurned the Jan 240s for 3 1/8, because the expiration date was only seven trading days away, on the 15th. Risk is one thing, suicide another. Because of the price, we bought only three calls for a total of $1,689 plus commissions (we don't like to spend much more than $4 or $5 per call, and these cost sufficiently more to make us economize).

The Feb 240s rose 1 point the next day on a 2 point gain in the OEX, a 19.2 point gain in the Dow, and a continued gain in volume. This looked too good to be true, since it had been going on for almost a week—four trading days. Gains in the Feb 240s were made on February 8, 9, 12 (Monday, even), not the 13 (a slight loss), February 14, when they were at 10 3/8, which meant we had almost doubled our money, the 15 (they were now at 14), the 16, and on into the month. On January 19 the Feb 240s were at 20, which means we were close to tripling our money. Should we take profit? We agonized and then laughed to the bank. Our $1,689 was now $6,000 (minus commissions) over a period of almost two weeks.

The next couple of days saw the market backing off a few points, but we were hooked. On Tuesday we entered another buy order. With the OEX at 257.69, we bought three Feb 260s at 4 1/4 each—against our principles, but we saw the saving of over $200 a contract and were misguided by it. The violation of principle was the buying of an out-of-the-money call rather than in-the-money, as principle has it. Why? We were confident of the market momentum carrying the day and were too penny wise and pound foolish.

Thursday was a big gainer, with the Dow up almost 52 points, the OEX up 6.35 and the Feb 260s at 8 1/2, so that in two days we picked up 4 1/4 points, or $1,275 ($425 times 3).

But the very next day saw a big drop of 44 points on the Dow and 4.47 on the OEX. We lost much of the previous day's gain. We believed that the market had more momentum, but we were no longer certain which way it would carry. For this was the famous January 23 that saw the market move between 2065 and almost 2220 with the OEX moving 14 points. It was a horrific day for the owner of options and we owned quite a few, including the three calls that rode up and down during the day, at one point with huge gains and again with sizeable losses. We were, frankly, too paralyzed to do anything, and probably wouldn't have been able to get the broker in any event. At the end, when the dust cleared away, the 260s were at 5 5/8, so we were still ahead.

By the following Wednesday the 260s were back at the 8 1/2 level. We had high hopes, since expiration was over three weeks away and we continued to believe that there was more gain in the market. We were encouraged by the fact that the huge move on January 23 now could be viewed as just a lot of program trading that had no effect at all on the general direction and thrust of the market. If you excised that day's trading on the chart, it was obvious that the direction was up, at least for the next few days. Or so it appeared on the charts.

By Wednesday, February 4, the Feb 260s were at 9 7/8. We took profits, for a total of about $1,689.

For the next two weeks or so the market fell into a trading range activity—good for combinations, bad for buying options. In the middle of February the market resumed its advance, and once again the buying of options seemed like an idea whose time had come. I call a move a "resumed advance" when: it has been going on for three days or more, the advance/decline line is favorable (many more advances than declines), the three component averages of the Dow move together, volume is either increasing or maintaining itself at an increased level from what went before (there are no absolute numbers), and the OEX index itself builds up volume or continues it. I should note also that because the OEX is composed of big capitalization stocks, it is important to take an occasional look at their fever charts, especially the stocks in the Dow.

On Tuesday, February 17, the OEX closed up over 6 points, at about 275. Anyone holding calls on that day would have made a handsome profit.

The Dow now stood at around 2240, and the main reason we were unwilling to enter earlier was that not all of our indicators noted above were present in a genial mode. For example, the utilities average declined the week ending February 6, while the others were advancing. But utilities resumed the week ending February 13. By the middle of the week the Dow components were back together in tandem advance.

With the OEX index at 275.79, the nearest in-the-money call was Mar 275 at 7. This seemed like a heavy premium to pay for an option only in-the-money by .79 or a little over 3/4 of a point. But we were convinced of market direction, and willing to risk 4 or 5 points. However, we bought only two OEX calls for $1,400. We don't, as a matter of principle, like to risk much more than $1,000 on option purchases.

The market began to correct over the next few days, and our Mar 275s dropped to 4 3/4, giving us a sharp loss. We returned to profitability March 5, just barely, when the Mar 275s moved to 7 1/8 under the stimulus of a Dow advance of 19 points. But time was wasting, along with our option. We decided to "roll up" the option. We cashed in the Mar 275s during the morning of March 6, at 7 1/4, which just about paid for commissions, and bought the April 280s for 7 1/2, thus building in a slight loss but buying four additional weeks' time.

Little action occurred through the following week. But on Friday, March 20, things looked up—up and away; the Dow moved up 34 points and the April 280s were now at 10 1/2. Looking back at our failed Mar 275s we saw sadly that had we held on to them we would have almost doubled our money by this surge on expiration date. They closed at 13 1/2. However, we had hopes, as usual, for April, even though it is "the cruelest month," according to T.S. Eliot. But what did he know about options? Indeed, on March 23, the market leaped another 30 points and our April 280s jumped to 14 5/8. It would have been wise to take profit—100 percent is always wise to take. But we are obstinate, not wise. We had over three weeks to expiration; we were willing to risk all, since we didn't have much at risk.

Risk turned to slight reward the next day, when the market moved up 5.40 on the Dow and our Apr 280s arrived at 15. A fall of almost 6 points in the Dow the following day reminded us that greed has few enduring attractions, however seductive it may be. Our call fell to 14 1/2.

Friday, March 27, was bloody. The Dow lost almost 37 points and the Apr 280s dropped to 9 3/8. We were submerged in gloom—and profit; we were still ahead of the game, handsomely. We tried to remember that the call had an April expiration on the third Friday. Thin reassurance of this sort is what rescues option players. We were no longer in a position of doubled profit, and now the prospect arose that if we continued to hold on to our stubborn position, we could very well lose, if not our shirt, at least our profits. But we held on; we were true believers.

The market did not oblige us on April 7; it dropped almost 45 points and chopped our cherry tree down—to 8 3/8. Though shell-shocked, we remained obstinate.

What happened the next day was a lesson in *Alice in Wonderland* market logic. The market went up 11.22 Dow points, the OEX .69, but our Apr 280s, down to 8 3/8 the day before, jumped to 11 1/4 on the .69 minuscule advance. The next day, on a Dow drop of 33 points, our Apr 280s collapsed anew, back to 7 7/8. From a position of doubled money, that we had recklessly squandered, we had arrived at cost—if we cashed in our chips on this day we would have barely covered costs. Now we faced the final week with the market in a full collapse. What to do? We had ignored telltale signals out of sheer obstinacy, and nothing more. When the market reached the 2400 plus mark, which we knew to be a target area of many market timing services, we should have taken our doubled money and departed. But we refused to accept reality and bulled ahead, senselessly. We woke up to this realization on April 13, when our Apr 280s had melted down to 2 1/8 from 15. Instead of buying the call back and rolling it in the direction it seemed most likely to follow, namely down, we decided to allow it, zombie-like, to run through to expiration, on a fool's hope. The market obliged us; on expiration date it ran up sharply and we extricated ourselves at 3 7/8, around mid-day. We were lucky; the market turned down at the close, ending about 7 points lower on the Dow.

The lesson is simple enough; take a good profit. We had doubled our money, but out of what the Greeks call hubris (arrogance against the gods), we had lost all of the profit and wound up losing half our investment. The dollar amount wasn't great, but everything else about our performance was a travesty of sensible procedure in these affairs. This lesson must be learned by everyone in the markets. Hubris should never control investment procedure.

High volatility and little sense of trend appeared to characterize the market in the early weeks of April. Yet if you looked back at the long view, you would see that the market had been going almost straight up from January 2 to March 23, when it embarked on a highly volatile correction, indeed almost a shoot-out. That was the Dow. The transportation and utilities averages were doing their own thing; utilities were diverging, as they had been doing since February; transportations were going sideways. These puzzling moves did not obscure the fact that the Dow, which is our basic point of reference, had been making a bottom of sorts—a double bottom, perhaps triple. Divergences may cause the "native hue of resolution to be sicklied o'er with the pale cast of thought," as Shakespeare observed about another gamble in *Hamlet,* but they should not cause you to take your eyeball off the ball, as Yogi Berra is supposed not to have said.

Out of both shell-shock and gloom, we saw no reason to buy any options for the nonce. But even beaten dogs return to a once meaty bone, not out of confidence, but perhaps from duty, blind faith or pure ignorance. Dog psychiatrists shed little light on these nuances, like market analysts studying my case.

As the Dow continued to drop over the next few days we realized that we had missed a golden opportunity to buy puts and put on a bear spread. When that happens—when it becomes clear that such an opportunity was going past in full view of your eyes and those of every market watcher from Chicago to Tokyo, and you missed it—the tactic is not to get mad but to get even. The way you do that is to *buy* options, especially if there are any signals from the market itself. There were such signs.

On April 15 the three Dow components, which were each doing their own, separate but equal thing, suddenly enlisted in the cause; they turned up, together, shouting nearer my profit to thee, in the words of the TV evangelist. We bought two calls, in wonder and hope, with the OEX index at 280; the Mar 285s at 5 3/4, cash on the barrelhead, costing $1,125 plus commissions. It was a lot of money at risk without the protections built into the combinations and hedges. But the market had dropped from 2430 down to 2215 (intraday), and we believed that enough was enough, already. In a word, the correction had had it. In situations like this, belief and hope intertwine, analysis and guess coalesce. One reason we believed the correction was either over or close to it came from what looked suspiciously like a triple bottom on March 13 and 27 and April 11. Three such tests of an intermediate low indicate that a great deal of money is betting on the buy side. It is not superstition but fact. When markets change direction it is caused by big sums of money coming in or departing. Volume on the three occasions noted was higher in two of the three cases. Higher means little between two consecutive days; it becomes important only on a trend, and in this case there were three successive days on which volume rose from the immediate period before, even though it wasn't a graduated rise. Increased volume is always an interesting and possibly important signal of market change. It isn't the only sign of change and it can be misleading, like all other signals and indicators. But it should always be taken into consideration.

For the next week or so nothing happened. On April 22 the market dropped 5 Dow points, the OEX dropped 1. It did little until April 29 when it moved up 22 Dow points with the OEX moving a tardy 2. The May 285s were 4 1/8. The Dow moved up 32 on April 30; the May 285s were now 5 1/4. On Tuesday, May 5, the Dow jumped almost 52 points, the OEX was up almost 7, and our May 285s were at 7 7/8, giving us a profit if we wanted it.

We took it, remembering our recent bout with hubris. We cashed in for a profit of 2 1/8 on two contracts, which came to about $400. The market next did an about face and headed down once again. Our triple bottom theory clearly wasn't to be borne out by events.

Buying OEX Options

The all-time best time to have bought OEX puts was in the period preceding the October 19, 1987 crash. But one of the best times to have bought calls was the next day, when the market shot up about 100 points and in fairly rapid order was soon destined to regain over half of the 508 point loss. That, of course, is hindsight. What should a rational approach be in any market situation of extreme volatility? That question, which we have been answering in various contexts throughout this book, might be answered generally like this. Summon every timing indicator you have knowledge of and faith in, and listen carefully to people with good records. Market timers are like baseball stars; they're streak hitters. Granville was unusually accurate before the bull market commenced in 1982. Many people predicted that the market was in for a king-sized correction in the summer and fall of 1987 and gave explicit reasons for it. A few even had the numbers more or less correct.

The problem with timing is that once you find indicators that work in one situation you rely on them when you don't notice that the situation has changed. In August and September of 1987 the market had reached new all-time highs and was starting down, in big leaps and small. But many people didn't believe what they were seeing. The market wasn't over-bought in September or early in October compared with June or July. The high price-earnings ratio (p/e) wasn't high in comparison with the numbers four or five months before (it was 22), and market veterans remembered such high p/e's in the past when no crash occurred. Also, in the weeks preceding the crash there was a lot of program trading and "portfolio insurance," which could have contributed to volatility even though nobody knew what to think about these new elements.

Market indicators are like military strategies used in the last war. They need to be adjusted subtly for changes that have occurred since the last time you depended on them and discovered that they worked—then. The psychology of overcoming false dependency is the most difficult art to master in the entire spectrum of investing. It isn't easy in any area. See Tennessee Williams' play *Streetcar Named Desire,* when Blanche is being led off to a mental hospital. She says "I have always depended on the kindness of strangers."

Hindsight is always despised on the false theory that everybody has it and what everybody has is contemptible. Everybody has eyesight but that doesn't prevent mistakes based on what you can see, nor does it simplify avoiding such errors based on eyesight alone. Every capacity can fail or be enhanced; the greatest home run hitter will one day be surpassed, the movie you now declare to be "the greatest" will be replaced by another, the "greatest pianist" will yield to someone yet unknown.

Until today, the greatest opportunity in buying OEX options occurred during the period just before, during and after the greatest (worst) market crash, which none of us is anxious to see surpassed but will certainly happen. That crash, October 19, 1987, was supposed to signal the onset of a terrible recession and a profound bear market. It did nothing of the sort. But it did a number of things that affected the OEX. The OEX was taking its lumps in the fateful summer of 1987, along with the general market.

The Dow had reached above 2760 in late August and then commenced its plunge. It had several notable drops, the biggest until then on October 14, a 95 1/2 point drop, followed on October 15 by a new record decline of 108 points. The *Wall Street Journal* attributed the drops to a "sharp rise in interest rates" and a roundup of a few of the other usual suspects, including the U.S. trade deficit. This kind of finger-in-the-wind reading can't be disproved and nobody will deny that raising interest rates poisons the market atmosphere. All these events, if combined with charts showing the inner workings of the market, did argue for a profoundly deteriorating market. The market had indeed been in a long, treacherous dropping pattern since August, and even if you weren't warned by the Declines of August, there was still time as late as the October 14 and 15 drops to do something about the stunning crisis of October 19 and its 508 point drop. You could have bought puts in plenty of time. It was highly rational to do so.

For example, at the close of the 95 1/2 point drop you could have bought November 290 puts for $5. Suppose you had spent $1,500 on three such puts. Monday morning's *Wall Street Journal,* written before the crash of that day, warned that "the bears are running wild," a fateful truth in a capsule headline. The Thursday plunge was followed by Friday's new record-setting loss of 108 Dow points. Your Nov 290 puts, for which you paid $5, were now worth $21. That's a gain of $1,600 for each of the three. At the close of trading, Monday, October 19 (the "crash"), the Nov 290 puts were at 103. Each put had appreciated 98 points or $9,800. Suppose you had bought twenty-five of them? That's almost $250,000.

More prudent types would not have waited so long to buy puts. You might have bought them soon after the record highs of August, in view of the enveloping gloom in Washington, Wall Street, and overseas. August puts would have enabled you to take advantage of at least half of the first 500 point decline from the 2760 highs.

All this, you say, is hindsight. But all of technical market analysis is based on hindsight and not all of it is wrong.

In a volatile environment you should do three things; buy puts and calls and use both bull and bear spreads. In the environment of July through December 1987, the bull and bear spreads would have worked much of the time; the buying of puts and calls would have worked throughout the period, depending on expiration dates, and how nimbly you reacted to events.

If you had held puts on the two big crises that occurred just before the 508 point crash, the chances are that you would have been tempted to take profits rather than risk a market turnaround. But on the actual day of the crash you would have been condemned to walk off with a full plate of profits; you wouldn't have been able to get through to your broker if you had been anxious to take profits at some point in the day. The phones were stoned. Brokers were either not answering or simply unable. So rapid was market movement that the entire system was overwhelmed. This part of it, we are assured, won't happen again.

In retrospect, it is easy to see that anyone buying calls the day after the crash, following the "bargain hunters" who came into the U.S. market from all over the world, could have made many OEX points. The market was up about 200 points in the first hour of trading, Tuesday morning, October 20, 1987. Selling then turned it around, but the market ended up over 100 points.

But what good is it to look in the paper afterwards and say you should have done this or that? Not much, yet such enormous moves—actually unprecedented so we cannot generalize too much—are invariably followed by opposite moves, though never of the same breadth and magnitude. We have had almost ten years of volatile markets, brought about by many factors, including computerization with all the attendant new market products that were made possible or called into being by the computer. Program trading, risk arbitrage, leveraged buyouts, vastly increased volume, the retreat of the small investor from the market, its increasing domination by the institutions (mostly huge pension funds), all played their roles in making the market ever more unpredictable and volatile.

These characteristics can be useful to skilled option players. Unfortunately, skill in option trading is to some extent like skill in human relations—"going with the flow," divining what to say and when. Or in Tom Wolfe's phrase "The Right Stuff." Wolfe was applying it to jet pilots and space pioneers, but options traders also need to be able to read signals that others don't see in highly stressful situations. Options exact stress and precision. I keep coming back to the baseball analogy; the difference between a .300 hitter and a .200 hitter—between enormous success and dismal failure—is the precise management of stress, all other things being equal. Reflexive response in baseball entails physical characteristics unrelated to market response, but doing the precisely correct thing under pressure is related to the options players. The OEX is a game as well as a market tool for speculators and investors. It is exciting, boring, frustrating and tense, sometimes all at once. I cannot overemphasize the right psychology involved in options, the absence of which means failure.

Usually the OEX trades in a range of less than 5 points in any given day. On big moves, up to 70 points in the Dow, it expands to a range of around 10 points. But on October 19,

1987, the OEX traded from a high of 274.13 to a low of 216 where it closed. That's a range of 58 points or over ten times the normal high range of 5 plus points. It was a dizzying, terrifying move, paralyzing most participants except those cool, exuberant customers who owned puts—a minority, but sizeable, since there was a total put volume of 145,701 on October 19 and a total put open interest volume (puts carried over) of 257,321. So, depending on entry point, several hundred thousand OEX players made money that day.

Am I saying that the price of success on a terrifying day was the ability to be calm and collected while everyone else was going crazy? Am I asking the impossible? No, only that you owned puts, based on analysis of the previous market trend, through the summer and into October. But that entailed saying "yes" to the buying of puts and, the next day, calls. Who could do that? Several hundred thousand investors and speculators, as we've noted.

All this relates especially to buying rather than to spreading or selling because statistics show that buying is a much riskier thing to do, even when you hedge. Hence the lecture on proper psychology and approach to it. When all is said and done, the market moves according to the psychology of the players. To be sure, I am talking about the big players, the fund managers—pension, mutual funds, etc.

Fast Forward in Time

It may be instructive to look at the period under discussion (December 1989 to February 1990) to see how buying OEX puts and calls relate. But first, it is well to reemphasize that special buying situations crop up all the time involving individual stock options. For example, everyone remembers the Bhopal, India disaster in which over 2,000 people were poisoned by gases from a Union Carbide factory. It may seem ghoulish to profit over a vast human tragedy, but markets conceal or diffuse all human relationships. It would be absurd to single out an isolated event in a million market-related events. Suppose I say "If I buy puts on Union Carbide stock and make a million I am doubly damned because I knew in advance I would make the money and knew the basis on which it would be possible." I could add "it is like insider trading, except that all of us are insiders and all should be prosecuted by an all powerful Rudolph Giuliani." He was a prosecutor before becoming mayor.

Bhopal was a very special situation; it turned out that Union Carbide, the corporation, had nothing to do with the tragedy. It was caused by a disgruntled employee. So any time you have a firm reason to believe that the stock of a company is about to plunge or fly, buy puts or calls on that stock. Financial markets are ethically neutral, like science. Nobody thinks we must banish science because it makes bombs as well as medicine.

It is actually much easier to guess an appropriate strategy for buying individual stock options when you read an article in the *Wall Street Journal* about some developing disaster in this or that company. It's inside information, all right, when the *Journal* is writing it up. The *Journal* has special sources, all legal, special knowledge, etc. When you read it, it could yet be inside information, depending on the time frame the article suggests for the disaster. But you must usually act quickly. The better the information (the more "inside" it is), the better off you may be, if you interpret the information correctly, and the market subsequently agrees with you. Everyone said that Exxon made a hideous error with the tanker Valdez. Exxon was banished into outer ethical darkness and the stock did decline several points. But business ethics and market interpretation are two different things. It has been said that much of what Ivan Boesky knew was based on hard, resourceful digging in unusual ways and places; he was doing what a research chemist, investigative journalist or physicist or geologist does in pursuit of their "inside" information, if you please, and mostly what he did caused the market to go up, hardly a crime except in the minds of federal prosecutors. (The Supreme Court refuses to define insider trading.)

However, the stock market shrugged off the tragedy of Valdez, and sent Exxon stock spiraling upward. (The courts punished Boesky, et alia, as if they had caused the Valdez disaster.) The initial shock of Valdez did indeed drop Exxon stock a few points, and had you bought puts on the stock you would have made gains. But not if you had held on. Then you would have made money only if you had sold your puts and bought calls. So the market must cooperate with your inside information and place the same directional value on it as you do. As to the ethical value of what you do, remember that all the great crimes against humanity in our century have come from crusaders who were bringing uplift and justice against oppression, so they said—Lenin, Stalin, Hitler. To be ethical in markets is to seek the truth in them and act accordingly. The truth in markets is to be found primarily in their internal relationships, not in the motives of the players, even though we admit that market psychology is the driving force. Motives of the players are simple enough to know; it's what happens once they act on motivation. All else is illusion or worse.

Every OEX trade, unless managed with care, has the potential to turn into a crisis. That is true even of the vertical spread, which is almost foolproof unless you have a fool for a broker who doesn't know what to do next, or in a crisis. A crisis in a vertical spread is defined as market movement against one of the legs of the trade, where your broker doesn't know what action to take or isn't around to take it.

The potential for crisis increases as the riskiness of your trading increases. One form of risk insurance is the buying of put-call spreads.

Every bull or bear spread should be accompanied by either the purchase of puts and calls or the opposite spread, if available. When you own a bear spread you should try to own a bull spread against it. If you own a bear spread on Monday with no bull spread available, keep trying. By Tuesday or Wednesday the bull will be there. But if it is not, then you must buy puts. That is what we now address.

Around the middle of December 1989, the market had recovered some equilibrium following its ascent back from the plunge of October 13, the 190 point quake. Thus it had a recovery of two months. We were now involved in vertical spreading which doesn't require any hedge; it has built-in hedges unless the market goes into crisis. Because crises are now a regular feature of markets, two or three times a year, it makes sense to consider the put-call spread as a hedge with every other OEX trade, excepting only the vertical spread.

In mid-December, because we were doing bull, later bear, spreading, we were in the put-call buying mood.

A chart of market movement showed an irregular ascent from the 2500 market where the market had landed with a thud, October 13, from a high of over 2800. A potential buyer of put-call spreads would have to decide where the market was going next, or if it was going anywhere. A decision is urgent; you want to weight the put-call spread in the right direction. If you think the market is going up you buy more calls, if down you go for puts. But if sideways you buy equal numbers of each.

Looking at the charts and looking at the news doesn't always offer conclusive evidence for your decision. We already had a bull spread in place in a bet on the customary Christmas rally, which was already in place. Santa Claus would be our market guru.

With the OEX at 331, and the rally looking healthy, we decided on January options. The Februarys were too expensive and we knew January would be a volatile month that could skew any prediction much beyond a week or two.

We bought the Jan 335s at 5. We bought a single Jan 325 put for 3 5/8. The three Jan 335s at 5 cost $1,500; the single Jan 325 put at 3 5/8 cost $362.50. Our motive was both to hedge our other strategies and to try to make a profit on these options.

The market proceeded to do nothing, or drop, over the next several days. On Monday, December 18, the OEX dropped 6 points and our single Jan 325 put went up from 3 5/8 to 7, or $700. Already we had guessed wrong. Had we reversed our buying—three puts to one call—we would have had puts worth $2,100 that cost about $1,000. Meanwhile, the calls were worth much less than we paid. With expiration four weeks away it was too early in the game to panic.

On January 2 the market leaped up and with it the OEX. It gained almost 7 points. The Jan 335s, which had slowly eroded in a side ways market, were brought back to what we paid for them, 5. The 325 put was 1 1/2, so we looked at a slight overall loss.

The market started dropping again, and our calls followed suit. On January 5, with a decline in the OEX of 3 points, the Jan 335s were a woeful 2 1/16. We decided it was time to cut our losses and switch to the put side. Both the Christmas rally and the January rally we hoped for and expected had other plans.

We took a 3 point loss on the three calls ($900) and bought two more puts and one call. We bought two 320 puts for 2 or $400 and one 340 call for 7/8 or $88. Expiration was January 19. Again, these were hedging and profit-seeking put-call buying spreads.

After several days of sideways movement the market took a sharp hit January 12. Our 320 puts were 5 3/8, giving us a profit of 3 3/8. The Jan 325 put that we had bought earlier for 3 5/8 was now 8 1/4. That meant we had a $462.50 profit on that single put and a $675 profit on the two 320 puts. We also had a slight loss on the single call. If we were willing to take profits we would have been even on our call buying. We held on. Hedging.

The OEX dropped another 2 1/2 points on Monday, January 15. Our 320 puts were unchanged; our 325 was at 9 3/8, or up over a point.

The market dropped sharply on Tuesday morning and we decided to cash in our puts. The 320s were at 6 1/4 when we sold; the 325 was at 10. Later in the day the market rallied and we thanked our good fortune and our broker who suggested getting out.

On the two 320 puts we made 4 1/2 points; we made 6 3/8 on the 325 put. That's $900 on the 320s, $639 on the 325, or $1,539 total. If the loss is subtracted, (the 3 calls times 3, or $900) we wound up with a small profit of $639, which is better than a loss.

But we also had a much more important item in the back of our wallet; throughout the time period discussed we had a hedge that would have made any huge market eruption highly valuable to us, whether up or down. We owned puts and calls. No such eruption occurred, but the age of program trading, like the age of aquarius, requires very precise safety measures, because you never know where or when trouble will start.

It goes without saying that the trader can add as many put-call OEX options as the wallet will bear.

On the next trading day, Wednesday, we looked at the put-call situation, which is always in flux like the river of Heraclitus (he said you can't step into the same waters twice, they were always changing; he had it right but he said it about 2000 years before stock markets). The OEX traded from a high of 321 to a low of 316 where it closed.

Was there any news? The economy was reported "not as weak as expected," which was interpreted on Wall Street as a tragedy of some magnitude, hence the market drop. The Dow had a drop of 33 points with a total of 94 in two days. A hundred here, a hundred there and soon you're talking real drop, as they say in Washington. Cyclical stocks, intimately related to boom and bust, such as IBM, Aluminum Co. of America, etc., took their cues and swooned ever so slightly.

OEX players need the big Dow stocks to reveal themselves fully since they control market direction, hence the OEX. Talk of weak corporate profits all over Wall Street, with consequent recession lurking in the wings, produced a streaky pessimism. Recession always makes the market go down; so does a lot of recession talk.

After a drop of 3 points, the OEX was at 317. The trajectory of the market was in a sharp, downward thrust, with some rise in volume over the past couple of days. These patterns characterized recent large market movements so we decided to continue to weight our trading to the bearish side. We bought three Feb 305 puts for $4 (i.e., $400 × 3). We bought, as a partial hedge, one 330 Feb call for $2 or $200. The date was January 18, 1990.

Our guess was wrong on the first day; the OEX traded up more than 2 points.

Our guess was right on the second day; on January 22 the OEX dropped about 9 1/2 points. The Feb 305 puts, bought for 4, were now at 6 1/4. The Feb 330 call, bought for 2, was at 1. So we had 2 1/4 points × 2 gain on the puts and 1 point loss on the call.

The next several days were not vitally eventful in the soap opera lives of our options. There was an event on Thursday, January 25, when the Dow dropped 44 points with the OEX dropping 4 at the close, but dipping lower than that earlier. Our Feb 305 puts were now at 7 (we paid 4). The lone Feb 330 call, bought for 2, was now 3/8. We thought, "that's okay, we'll keep it as a hedge." Only $200 was invested in it. We held our puts.

On January 26 the OEX traded down during the day sufficiently to send our $4 puts (Feb 305s) to $7.50. We took it, turning $800 into $1500. We continued to hold the solitary call. Why cash in when our downside prediction seemed to be going our way and we might have come away with higher profits? In options you take profits; losses are ever waiting to take you (to the cleaners).

We were puzzled by the market. It was at the 2550 level, which technicians viewed as an important bottom. We were leery of too enthusiastic an interpretation of our success. The moment you begin to believe in your own market wisdom there is an almost certain guarantee that you will regret it shortly. So, because the period had been short and painless, the profits though small were encouraging. Had I been a gambler—and the true OEX player has a gambler's instinct to go with his information—I would have bought about twenty puts instead of two.

We fretted over the market for the next day or two, then, on January 31, a sharp move upwards began. We decided to go with that flow. We bought two calls (to go with our Feb 330) and one Feb 300 put. We paid $3 for the put and $2.50 each for two Feb 315 calls. In other words, we were now betting on a market bounce. We were also hedged in case of a market crisis.

On Friday, February 2, the market traded up and the OEX went up as much as 4 points, but didn't hold on to all of it. At the close the OEX was up almost 2 points. We held.

On February 5, the next trading day, the OEX moved between 310 and 308.

A rally occurred February 7, with the OEX closing up 5 points.

The Feb 315 calls, bought for $2.50 each, were, alas, only at $3.00. Ours not to reason why, ours but to hold and sigh.

Expiration was little more than a trading week away, on February 16. We faced losses across the board. The calls were going nowhere, the put was dead. To be sure, our losses wouldn't amount to much, but they would nullify our gains elsewhere. That's the ever present danger in OEX trading. But the principle of the three-ring circus trading menu we have enunciated remains a useful one. You need a repertory of tactics in OEX trading that always contains puts in a market going down or calls going up, to cope with market crises—any market that moves more than 75 points (my definition).

CHAPTER 7

Futures Trading:
The S&P 500

Stock Index Futures—Where They Fit in

Stock index futures, better known as the S&P 500, are financial futures instruments or commodities. They differ in most ways from the options on the S&P 100 we deal with primarily. However, they do reflect the New York stock market, like the OEX. And settlement is in cash, as with the OEX. But their behavior otherwise is more akin to financial and other commodities than to options. Their use in our OEX strategies is as a supporting instrument, rather than as the main event.

This may seem odd, since there are brokers who do nothing but trade the S&P 500 futures, as there are many individual speculators who also concentrate on it to the exclusion of all else. Here we are asking you to master it along with the different skills we've covered thus far. Admittedly, it isn't essential, and it adds an element of risk not otherwise present. It also adds a certifiable amount of margin requirement as with combination selling. So that is another count against it. Moreover, we recommend its use infrequently. In fact, we recommend it as often as we recommend the buying of puts and calls and for the same reason; as a method of profiting on spectacular market moves.

I would not recommend trading S&P 500 futures in a market as volatile as the October 1987 one (when margin costs rose to $20,000). You should wait, instead, for the market to return to a more normal pattern.

In this chapter we will cover market conditions for trading these futures, keeping losses to a minimum, finding indicators, avoiding false signals, and when to trade and when not to trade. We will also discuss brokers and what you should expect from them. Though our interest in the S&P 500 futures index is an occasional one, the information in this chapter will enable you to trade it exclusively and regularly, if you so desire.

In 1980 the Chicago Mercantile Exchange published a book explaining the forthcoming S&P 500 stock index futures, stressing four aspects: 1. The S&P 500 futures index could serve as a hedge for use by commercial traders to protect against possible loss due to fluctuations in stock prices. 2. It could serve as a societal benefactor in that it would generate new price information, thus adding to the total available amount. 3. It would enhance "prospects for equity financing by corporations." 4. It would promote capital formation "in the long run by reducing the risk of corporate bankruptcy throughout the economy."

No claim was made that it will reduce highway accidents, wars, depressions and civil strife.

Without tracing each argument in detail, one may note that the only conspicuous use of these futures has turned out to be that of arbitragers in program trading. Program trading may be a form of hedging, of course, but whether it has any relation to the other three justifications above is unclear. Also, it is unclear as to how one might go about finding out. In any case, there is no need to analyze the genealogy of its use, but it is

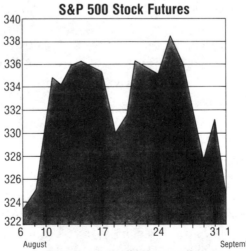

The S&P 500 stock index futures leap around like gazelles, as this Chicago Mercantile Exchange graph shows in a mere three-week charting.

important to master the use of it, since profit can be derived, and losses, too. A case can be made for individual improvement in finances, if the index is used profitably, no matter whether corporate America uses it or not. If you look at the numbers involved in it, however, the public is *not* using it. On a day when there were one million open contracts in the OEX, there were about 93,000 in the 500 index. So it is a highly elite clientele addressed by the contract and is perhaps what the Chicago Mercantile Exchange had in mind.

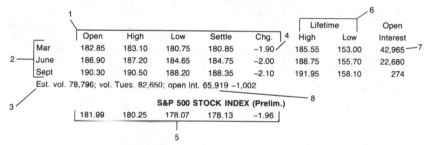

FUTURE PRICES
S&P 500 FUTURES INDEX (CME) 500 Times Index

	Open	High	Low	Settle	Chg.	High	Low	Open Interest
Mar	182.85	183.10	180.75	180.85	−1.90	185.55	153.00	42,965
June	186.90	187.20	184.65	184.75	−2.00	188.75	155.70	22,680
Sept	190.30	190.50	188.20	188.35	−2.10	191.95	158.10	274

Est. vol. 78,796; vol. Tues. 82,650; open int. 65,919 −1,002

S&P 500 STOCK INDEX (Prelim.)

| 181.99 | 180.25 | 178.07 | 178.13 | −1.96 |

1 Prices represent the open, high, low, and settlement (or closing) price for the previous day.
2 Contract delivery months that are currently traded.
3 The number of contracts traded in the previous two trading sessions.
4 Change from the previous day's settlement price.
5 The actual index open, high, low, close and change.
6 High and low prices over the life of the contract.
7 The number of contracts still in effect at the end of the previous day's trading session. Each unit represents a buyer and a seller who still have a contract position.
8 The total of the right column, and the change from the prior trading day.

Trading prices are disseminated instantaneously throughout the world by the various quotation transmission services, and are carried daily in the business pages of most major newspapers. This is how one major newspaper lists the daily displays of S&P 500 stock index futures trading. To convert the quotations below to dollar value, simply multiply the quote by $500. For example, a short position in the March S&P 500 futures contract, held from the prior day through the close of trading with a change of −1.90, would be credited with a 1.90 × $5 or $950 profit.

*Reprinted from "Using S&P Stock Index Futures and Options" published by the Chicago Mercantile Exchange.

S&P futures are magic, incantatory formulas known as financial futures. They do not foretell the future; they can ruin it without relating to it. They are dangerous and opportunistic. We know them only as blips on a computer screen. We do not understand why they are there. We know little of what they represent, what they mean, if they mean anything. We think we know what the stock market means. We may also believe that we know what the OEX means in that both translate into trading vehicles attached to U.S. industry, commerce, government and politics.

Some analysts deny that such a connection exists between markets and the real world. But it took the human race more than 100,000 years to discover the relationship between childbirth and sexual intercourse. Cause and effect lags are not an unusual feature of human awareness. They are especially conspicuous in financial affairs.

But is it necessary to know precisely what happens behind each blip in the S&P 500? No. First of all, nobody except the Chicago Mercantile Exchange knows, and they aren't saying though they are talking. You can trace an order back to the source that accepts it, including your broker, his contact on the floor of the futures index pit, and so forth, and the contract that is expressed by your order and payment, as well as the margin payment to your broker. If you ask any of these individuals what these events mean you will hear an answer like "It's making a market," but if you ask, "A market in what?" the answer will be vague and inconclusive, or circular—a market in financial futures is apt to be the end of it.

However, we do know the consequences of setting a contract in motion, just as doctors know how to prevent some diseases without knowing why, and that is what interests us.

Whatever else they are, stock index futures are instruments of arbitragers, who buy stocks and sell the futures, or sell stocks and buy the futures. These stocks are members of the S&P 500, the big cap stocks that comprise the backbone of the NYSE and indeed the U.S. economy. They don't leap around in the daily standings. Many of them pay large dividends, which also keep their volatility low. But the S&P futures index that is based upon them is just about the most volatile single item you can trade, even more so than the S&P options, which are volatile enough. So their temperament is the opposite of what they are based upon, and anyone intending to trade them, thinking of the old reliable S&P 500 in their title, should think again.

The S&P futures are neither old nor reliable; they are new and reckless and should be used sparingly, if at all. At first they were aimed at fund managers and institutional traders of all stripes, who scorned them, perhaps out of unfamiliarity or caution. Things have changed, though not entirely, and their chief users are the big arbitragers whose tactics send the market up and down with such speed and force.

Big trader tactics can be inferred to some extent by monitoring the relationship between the stock index futures and their cash index—today's price of the S&P 500 index. These two prices appear to have some independence, but when the daily cash index is below the price of the futures index significantly (there is no set number or ratio; it depends on individual fund managers), the buy programs are set in motion. But when the cash index price rises above the futures index price, the sell programs are activated. The signal is not unerring because it depends again on the judgments of the big fund managers.

The problem of monitoring the S&P 500 futures remains attention span and availability of data. How much watching and thinking can you do when your money is at stake. Where can you watch? When? If you are uncomfortable with the answers to such questions, it is best to locate a broker who specializes in these contracts.

This chart illustrates the convergence of the index futures price and the underlying cash index. The gray band describes the various arbitragers' transactions costs, and defines the "fair value" futures price. Any futures price outside the gray band represents arbitrage opportunity.

Going for Brokers

Brokers are people who sell financial instruments. They are indispensable, but their expertise may be expensive. The more you can substitute your own knowledge for theirs, the better off you will be, financially and, possibly, emotionally. Brokers are often busy—and rich. Unless you are a big investor or trader you won't attract much of their attention as they cheerfully accept your orders.

Brokers analyze market direction, or read what their analysts say, and select various investment categories, matching stocks, bonds, and so forth, to customers, especially if the customers are important to them. Most people won't rate the highly personalized attention required for profitable trading in the S&P 500 futures. As a result, most investors will lose money or make less than might be expected. That isn't because brokers are dishonest (some are), but what they sell to you may be inopportunely timed or may be an in-house "float" that they are stuck with that seemed such a great deal when the house took it in, like an appealing cat. Also, brokers' recommendations don't come from outer space; they come from the house research department, and many brokers are on their own, especially in such specializations as options and stock index futures.

Brokers go to work each day to trade—no trades, no commissions. But conditions for trading stock index futures do not occur every day. Indeed, the worst single mistake is too-frequent trading, or lack of discipline. Because that is both psychological and real, such trading is not always easy to avoid. One may be too easily trapped into trading, from panic or greed, or the mistaken view that after a few successful trades you have mastered the tricks of this particular trade. If you are ever overcome by such pleasant delusions, it is vital to stop trading.

Because stock index futures move rapidly, especially in a volatile market, it is usually important to take every profit possible. Brokers may be too busy to execute such a program, despite your self-interest in the matter, and theirs too.

There is also the problem of telephonitis and broker behavior. Let me illustrate. My broker, at one of the world's largest houses, espoused an interesting system of day trading, dipping in and out of the market two or three times a day, at $35 a crack, when the S&P futures began trading and I was an interested trader.

Day trading is a roll of the dice. Your broker doesn't mean to impoverish you, as he rakes in his fees, but the odds are usually against you. He would indeed rather enrich you, but there is a pecking order to enrichment. He deals primarily with the goose that lays most of his eggs—his $100,000 plus accounts. When you sashay in with a $10,000 or even a $6,500 account, which he will take holding his nose the while, you may be distraught to learn how easy it is to run through your cuddly nest egg, while he is buttering up the gotrocks goose to keep that creature laying the truly golden eggs. So, one day in September 1982, with the birds (and the market) flying south, we agreed (reluctantly) to sell an S&P futures short, just as I was watching the market begin a turnaround to go up. Ah well, markets go down as often as up, and no trend was established with any certainty. It was touch and go; he had touched base with me and I agreed to go. We were stopped out within minutes, losing $600 or $700. The day wore on and I called him, reaching him with difficulty. I did not blame him for that. It was, after all, a new account and a new product. Neither of us had any inkling of the long shadow it would cast over the stock market.

In our conversation he argued and I agreed that the market was going nowhere (at the particular time). Suddenly at 2:20 the market began to take off in flight; the TRIN was dropping rapidly, a guarantee that big buying was coming in, and the Dow was moving up equally rapidly. I called, urgently wanting him to buy a long contract. He was out to lunch; the S&P futures index went through the ceiling. I lost not only the $600 or $700 I was anxious to recoup from earlier in the day, but an additional $2,000 or more profit while he was out to lunch. I hope he was at a French four-star restaurant.

I had other dismal experiences with brokers who assured me that their systems were foolproof, including one now famous discount broker who declared in early August 1982, the start of the biggest bull market in history, that Joe Granville was correct, that the market was about to drop from 800 to 500 or lower (Granville's most infamous market call).

Thus the price charged for transactions, whether at full-service houses, or the newest discount company, is no guarantee that you won't lose your money.

The brokers I mention are not necessarily typical, and they may not even be the worst. But they were ignorant of what they were selling and doing—parading under false pretenses, if you will, yet no jury in the land would convict them. On the contrary, one of them is now rich, with his own firm, the other not poor. The now rich broker assured me that while my loss of $700 was regrettable, he was nevertheless "Glad I made the trade; it showed me something about the market." His education, which I scarcely needed, stood him in little stead. A week later he made an exactly similar mistake.

I cite these dismal anecdotes to warn you against brokers who may dangle alluring promises at you. Ask them for a written record of what they have done lately. It is important that it be recent, because brokers, like big league batters, go in streaks, and you want a winning streak. Do not sign up with a broker who has only a failing record to show you.

Keys to S&P Trading

The keys to S&P trading are more immediate than the economics, politics and other non-market events that intrude throughout the day. They involve, first of all, two questions: who is doing it, you or a broker, and on which machinery is it being done? If you deal through a broker you are in trouble unless you have a viewing terminal at the broker's office or in your own home, though the cable TV Financial News Network will do. Too many brokers will lack the expertise and time to provide the right trading insight, and there is a fundamental divergence between your interest and his; on most days you will not trade the S&P futures index, whereas brokers are in business to trade. It's like generals and wars. Trading the S&P is only in your interest when an emphatic trend can be discerned. How you do that will be explained insofar as possible, but brokers have little interest in trends that don't induce buyers to come to market. Yet trading only on trends—up or down—is the only way to succeed, both in stock index futures and options too, though we know about all the exceptions (combinations, for one). The point is there are no exceptions with the index futures; they work only in a trending market, up or down.

Trend analysis involves questions on the method of analysis. Is it to be both technical and fundamental or one or the other? It should indeed be both, but if you deal with a broker you are at the mercy of his particular bias. It can be fatal to your prosperity, not his; he wins every time.

Are your losses thus inevitable? They are inevitable, yet they needn't be large. They are mostly yours to control. Stop-loss orders are essential, if temptation overcomes better judgment and you find yourself trading too often. Financial parameters should be established at the start. The basic contract requires that you put $6,500 up front (margin). If you master the S&P futures index you can add as many contracts as your profits allow. But you should use stop-loss orders so that you never lose more than about $300. At the other end of the spectrum, you have to learn to leave a profitable trade. The S&P can turn against you even in the most favorable markets. Such markets are not all that common.

Market direction and movement are the two basic keys to assess, both in daily and longer-term trading. The first key to all market behavior is volume—up or down. There may be large moves in the Dow averages on moderate volume, but it is rare that such volume will produce the right market chemistry for the moves needed in profitable S&P trading.

Trading Tactics

While all commodities have some things in common in their trading and goals, the key difference between the S&P index and other commodities is that it is based on the NYSE and represents about 80 percent of the value of all issues traded there. Because the stock market in turn represents U.S. industry and commerce, the S&P reflects corporate America. As we have seen, it comes to us with many claims by the Chicago Mercantile Exchange that it will aid U.S. corporations to raise capital, and that it will enable individual investors to hedge their portfolios, among other things.

When the S&P index started to trade, it was a mystery to everyone because of its differences. When its volatility became clear, it was a deeper puzzle because its trading looked like nothing so much as the rapid patterns of pork bellies, and what had bacon to do with 80 percent of corporate America?

Because the opening price of the S&P is based on the opening prices of T-bonds and bills, traders soon commenced watching the daily movements of these financial futures. They remain among the leading indicators of direction for the S&Ps. One trades warily in the S&P against the direction of the Treasury issues. Because the Kansas City Value Line and the New York futures indexes move in the same direction as the S&P, but at a different pace and range, they also became points of reference.

Many indicators enable us to track daily trading in the S&P index. But what if you decide to buy or sell a contract with the intention of holding it for a long market move up or down? The only indicators are the various short term inferences we may make—the clues we select to track. These are both technical and fundamental and are no mystery—the usual advance/declines, oversold/undersold conditions, and so forth. But holding a long or short contract over time takes nerves of steel; it is recommended only for people able to withstand heavy losses, since a single day's trading in one contract can gain or lose up to $3,500, if you own the contract from the opening bell and hold it throughout the trading day. And if the market goes against you for a few consecutive days your losses can become enormous.

All trading has its risks, but stop-loss orders can help to minimize them. You cannot expect to catch many $3,500 days, using a day trading system, but there can be many days that will net from $500 to $2,000 per contract.

The Start

Stock index futures commenced trading in early 1982, with the Kansas City Value Line index, which is based on the 1700 or so stocks tracked by Value Line. The Value Line service had nothing to do with it, but that old-line investment service, with its somewhat conservative format, profited enormously from association with the high flying index. The S&P futures index arrived in April 1982, and soon became the most popular of the stock index futures. Next came the New York Stock Index. Though its initial fee was about half that of the other two— about $3,500—it did not achieve the popularity of the S&P 500. Based on the Big Board stocks, it moved more slowly. Its rewards and losses were half those of the other two, and it failed to achieve much popularity. The Major Market Index Futures appeared later, based on twenty New York stocks.

These indexes move more or less in tandem, but the Value Line moves more quickly and often (but not always) shows the direction for the others. We will concentrate on the S&P 500.

Note that there are 20 "ticks" in each 100 points of these contracts; each tick is worth $25, and the ticks sometimes move with ferocious quickness. So each 100 points equals $500, 200 points equals $1,000, and so on.

The average amount of trading back in 1982, on a day when the market moved up or down by 5 to 10 points on the Dow, was about 300 points up or down, or 150 up and 150 down on a day when no emphatic trend developed. Things have changed; the market no longer moves 5 or 10 Dow points on an average day. It is more apt to move 30 to 50 points, and throughout the year will move 100 points or more on several explosive days. The problem with these explosive days is that they are unpredictable, even to the most successful methods of market analysis. They make hash out of the best market system, no matter how carefully designed and executed it might be.

Does this mean that the sideways market is finished and with it our combination strategy? Does it also mean that S&P trading is too dangerous because it cannot cope with such explosive days?

These questions can't be answered conclusively since their answers will vary with individuals who trade and who continue to succeed—or fail. Climactic market peaks that send the Dow up or down in huge swings reflect major money commitments by the big fund managers. Yet they do not command limitless funds, nor are their major trading decisions undertaken in a vacuum. Big fund managers operate under constraints like anyone else; their performance is monitored relentlessly. They do not make investments in the wrong market environment. Yet they continue to use these risky instruments.

What about the arbitragers who manipulate the markets with their stock index futures play? Most days on which program trading erupts and sends the Dow up or down dramatically are not days on which the major trend is disturbed or changed. So the most rapidly moving Dow day is not based on market trend so much as on market accident, e.g., what ever causes the change in the relationship between the S&P 500 cash index futures price and the price of the S&P 500 cash index, and whatever else causes the major fund players to undertake the moves they make. The one cause is mathematical, the other psychological.

Thus there are no easy answers to the questions posed above. Mathematical models are subject to interpretation; psychological dilemmas cannot be fathomed precisely.

Perhaps the most difficult problem with the S&P 500 is getting out of it. When the market is moving quickly, the release of your contract can become tricky. Assume that the market is going against you, as it will do each and every day at some time or other—a sobering fact if facts do induce sobriety in you (with some people it's coffee or nothing). You must have a stop-loss order built into every contract you assume, even though the order is in effect an extra contract ($15 to $35 or whatever) and even if floor traders look upon a stop-loss order derisively.

If the market isn't moving quickly one needs no stop-loss order. Then it's easy, or should be, to quit a bad trade. Say you bought a contract at 9:30 a.m., and by 10:30 the market moves decisively the other way; it commences falling rapidly. You, a day trader, need a good night's sleep, and have little need to lose a lot of money. You simply sell back the contract you bought, taking your loss (or buy back the contract you sold). On a single contract you should aim at avoiding losses above $250 or $300, meaning 12 ticks. Isn't that unrealistic, given the speed of the passing tick parade? Yes it is unrealistic, once the market begins a major move, but it is the only saving grace for the trader, whose primary motivation is the saving of his skin. Skin-thin psychology is endemic to this kind of trading.

The long-term trader of the S&P 500 has a different time frame and psychology (and bank balance) in mind. That person aims at taking advantage of trends, not ticks, using stop-loss orders more sparingly. Instead of a stop-loss order twelve ticks above or below your contract price, you might double the distance and loss risk on the assumption that a swing in one direction will be corrected by the next swing. Is such an assumption rational? Often it is, though no statistics support it unfailingly.

Quitting a profitable trade is an important part of the learning tree. Greed contends with reason, intoxication with sobriety. You attribute your successful trade to your own powers of analysis and methodology, requiring only that you continue on the same path. But a good profit is no respecter of persons, especially one in whom greed has become the key motivation. The next step becomes the snatching of loss from the jaws of profit. At the market's present stage—in the 2200 to 2400 range—a 200 S&P point move is about the norm. That's a move of $1,000. Usually such moves are followed by retracements, both more or less. Day traders will cash in such a move, then set another contract (or contracts) in the opposite direction. It's highly risky; highly profitable *if* and only if you can learn to do it.

If you don't go in for day trading, in which you are out of the market at the end of each day, you needn't worry about minute-by-minute indicators. What you do worry about is market direction, as with stocks and options.

The S&P consists mostly of big stocks comprising about 80 percent of the total value of all stocks on the NYSE. Their movement does not necessarily correspond to the rest of the market precisely, but the S&P 500 is extremely sensitive to the trading index or TRIN that measures the constant ebb and flow of buying and selling, throughout trading. It is measured numerically by upticks versus downticks (buys versus sells). When they are about equal, the number of the TRIN is 1.00. As the balance tips, according to the flow of orders, the number reflects market direction. If the market goes up the TRIN number goes down and vice versa. But market direction is all important. The TRIN may be a trend follower at any given moment—the time it takes the specialist or market maker to sort out the orders—as well as a trend initiator. The TRIN can be in bear market territory, around 1.20, for example, when suddenly the S&P 500 can turn and commence a strong upward movement, turning into a bullish move even while the Dow is in negative territory and the advance/decline ratio (the number of advancing versus declining stocks) is yet in favor of the losers.

The TRIN reflects what is going on in the big actors of the NYSE drama. Just as IBM and General Motors can have a crucial effect on the market as a whole, so they and their fellow big capitalization stocks can move the S&P 500 index around in midstream, turning bear into bull and vice versa.

Note that though the S&P 500, the Value Line, and the other stock indexes are more or less alike in their behavior, they are not identical. The Value Line is more volatile because it contains a lot of smaller ASE and OTC stocks along with big capitalization NYSE members. While the Value Line index appears to move first, and it must always be consulted before you make a move, it does not always predict the next direction of the S&P 500. When markets rise the S&P rises more rapidly, and the converse is always true, while the NYFE index moves less rapidly, as you might expect from an index based entirely on the Big Board.

Market Timing and the S&P

Thus far we have indicated general approaches toward the trading of S&P 500 futures. Now let us look more closely.

The best way to approach market timing and direction is to have the right computer program, keyed into all the market fundamentals we've been discussing. These also include such technical procedures as cycle charting of various types, which are as "fundamental" to market movement as war and peace, the economy, leading indicators, and so forth. Charts reflect the buying and selling by millions of investors, but they also reflect who is buying what and for how much. Charts, after all, are kept on individual stocks.

If you have a home computer you need a program that keeps you informed about two kinds of information: news from the Federal Reserve Board that affects markets (any announcement from Washington having to do with financial circles, for example news about oil prices and taxes), and then all the specific market-moving news generated by the market itself (volume, TRIN advance/declines, the other futures index contracts, especially Value Line and the NYFE, also the Dow, the transportation and utilities indices, the ASE and OTC data stream, the relation of the cash market S&P 500 to its futures, and the similar relationships on the Value Line index, the put-call ratio, the cycle charts of three, ten and thirty day moving averages). All these components of ebb and flow in markets must be kept front and center, available to you instantly throughout the day's trading—or to your broker, who has agreed with you on their use in S&P futures trading.

You may throw up your hands in horror and say "impossible." But if you can get it all on a computer screen, properly organized, you can master it with a little practice.

Don't trade S&P (or other) futures on a day when the signals are mixed. Ideally, the NYSE, ASE and OTC markets should move in tandem, up or down. Once this condition is met, the most favorable signals for buying an S&P futures contract (going long) are: a TRIN below 70 and falling; and the Dow moving up powerfully (for example, up 35 in the first half hour or so), allowing for a pullback that doesn't exceed more than half of the rise. Look for market barriers and resistance points. If the Dow approaches one of the psychological barriers, as they are termed—2000, 2200, 2300, 2400—where automatic sell or buy signals are activated, you can expect a sharp reaction in the S&P, both in the spot or cash index and in the futures. Get out of the market when this happens, unless all other signals beckon otherwise.

The computer can summon indicators instantly, so long as you have the right program punched in and it is available. If you're trading at a brokerage firm or calling in to a discount house, you will be at a big disadvantage, especially at the discount house. They can't afford to coddle you with information. At present there are only two alternatives to use these futures for your own profit; one is through the home computer that is correctly programmed, and the other is at a brokerage firm where the computer programs are made available to the amateur trader. You will pay more at the brokerage house, but if the information is available, you will also make more. Ultimately, the best arrangement is the home computer (and a schedule that allows you to use it).

There are brokers who do specialize in the S&P 500 futures index (and the NYFE and Value Line), and if you can locate such an individual who will show you his or her track record, and you like what you see, then I cannot logically urge you to do anything except use that broker. But do not use a broker who isn't a specialist in stock index futures. A commodities generalist will generally lose your money; he or she cannot possibly have the time, resources and information to trade these contracts profitably along with all the other commodities.

In the morning, when trading commences, you will be puzzled at what happens to the S&P 500 futures price. Before the opening, the price will appear on the boards as the previous day's closing price. But the new price is what the mercantile exchange market makers declare it to be, usually based on what the interest sensitive commodities (financial futures) are doing. If they open sharply up or down, so will the S&P 500 futures index, simply because that is the way the market makers think the market will go, at least for a while or until order flow takes over. If the financial futures open unchanged or near that, don't expect much change in the S&P futures. In any event, what happens after the opening depends next on the NYSE almost entirely, unless there is no movement in the 500 stocks, which is unlikely. Then there may be a temporary lull in the futures index.

If then the S&P (and the other index futures) show a tendency to move, and the Dow Jones Industrials also show movement, don't be tempted into the market without confirmation from all other sources, as outlined above. Over half the time, the S&P index will swing up and down 100 points or more in the first hour, and if you want to trade you must be extremely nimble—or foolhardy. Sell short when the S&P tops out, long when it bottoms out. This can happen within a few minutes. How do you know? When the TRIN stalls and reverses, that's one almost unerring sign. Others: When the OTC and ASE markets move into synchronization after disagreeing earlier; when the spot indexes of all the futures change direction, and the advance/decline ratio changes direction, as shown by a change from negative ticks to positive or positive to negative, or perhaps where some news item from a market-moving source comes into play.

A market that starts the day with low volume, with indecisive trading index (the TRIN around 1.00), with financial futures neither up nor down by more than a few points, is a market that offers nothing to the day trader at that time. But some days that start without a primary trend may develop one that is sufficiently strong to trade later on, especially in the last hour. Since the S&P trades for fifteen minutes after the rest of the markets close, the last hour should be watched with special care. If at 2:15 p.m. the S&P suddenly springs into action out of lethargy, don't hesitate; follow its direction and buy or sell a contract (or however many you trade). It is important to take advantage of any friendly market movement, since most days are unfriendly—they vacillate or thrash around indecisively.

Indecisive markets are far more common than those that move as part of a major trend. That is why the S&P index is not to be traded frequently, even by day traders.

Consider that the 500 index, on December 31, 1986, stood at 260, the cash index at 259. On January 2 the market began the move that carried it from Dow 1900 to 2400. A trader who was not in this market would have lost a major opportunity, both in bull spreads and the S&P 500 index (to say nothing of buying calls). Using these tactics in combination would have been one of the best episodes in the bull market that began in 1982. It was one of the rare episodes in which all of our strategies converged.

We bought a single 500 index contract early on in the January rush. But one needn't have caught the very first day, January 2, in order to profit enormously. Even if you had owned only one 500 index contract when the index was well above the 260 level, and had held on through most of the rally, you would have profited enormously. Suppose you waited a week or ten days to make certain that the rally was no fluke and had bought one contract at 270. By May 8 it was about 295, which would have given you 25 points. Each point is worth $500, so you would have been ahead $12,500 for a single contract that cost you about $6,000 (margin cost, but still your money). Rich traders would have added contracts when it became clear that the movement was a powerhouse.

Had you not caught the move at 270, but at (say) 280, you would have done well—15 points, or $7,500. But suppose you became intoxicated with your own success—the Stalinist syndrome—and held on, thinking there was no end. There was; by May 21 the index was at 280, and sinking.

Once the market took off on its January rally, there was no question that we were in for another big upward move. All the important market timers were calling for such a move and our signals were united; the volume was friendly, the trading index and its moving average were in strong buy territory, the big fund managers were buying (block trades going by on the tape and individual stocks were showing big volume gains), the three parts of the Dow were going in the same direction, and in a word, the bells were ringing, the bull roaring. So, bold traders, restless for more opportunity than buying calls and bull spreads, would have bought at least one S&P 500 futures contract.

Risks and Rewards

What about the risks and rewards of day trading through such a period? Risks are obvious and plentiful, rewards possible but far from guaranteed, despite the upward sweep of the Dow.

From January 2 through January 22, anyone holding a contract in the 500 index would have had difficulty losing money, since the market went almost straight up. January 23 was the inevitable day of reckoning. On that day the Dow opened at 2158.46 and moved up to 2185.48, in an apparent continuation of the big January rally. Volume was record-breaking, signifying to the unwary that the bull rush might well make new highs and records of several sorts. It did, but the wrong ones. Profit-taking came in like a tornado. On a volume of over 300 million shares, the Dow collapsed in the last three hours, dropping 44.15 points on the day. As it had been as high as 2210 and as low as 2060 (approximately), it dropped a total of about 150 points before "recovering" to a drop of a mere 44 points. Had you been a holder of a long S&P futures contract you would have been a big loser during the day, assuming that you would have been unable to get out before that. In such a trading day, loss-limit orders or stop-loss orders are often ineffective because of the crush of orders, and the chances are that you would not have gotten out without sizeable losses. On the other hand, you had enormous gains.

Had you been only in stocks or bonds, or the owner of both puts and calls, you would have had few if any losses. Stocks don't move a great deal during such days, bonds never move much, and puts and calls balance out or leave a slight gain or loss. Hedging tactics don't work as well with the S&P 500 index, unless you are an institutional trader with a lot of them in your portfolio. If you have a long and short contract (one each), they will cancel each other out on the same move. They don't offer the possibility of one side being a big winner, the other a small loser, as with a put-call combination, unless you have two contracts, one of which makes a much bigger move than the other. But that's too risky a game.

So if all is risk what is the point of it? Some traders have shown the point, for example, the Davis-Zweig report, which has a notable record of profit. If you trade only on those few days throughout the year when all the signals are clear and unequivocal, you can also be a big winner. It's when you begin to think that you can trade any or every day, at the seductive behest of someone else, or your own ego, that it is time to call a halt or quit altogether.

The Trades

The huge January to April 1987 move from 1900 to 2400 stalled and retraced, as we've noted. During the last week of April 1987, the market was apparently recovering some poise from the 200 point drop that had begun during the first week. The question always arises in such a sequence: is it time to get aboard? Perhaps for a bull spread, yes, but the S&P index is a touchier device. On April 23 the futures index, June contract, had a trading spread between 291 and 284, which means that had you sold short at 291 and bought the contract back at 284, you would have gained 7 points or $3,500 on a single contract. What would your chances be of catching such a move? Virtually nil. It is true that the market dropped 30 points by noon, after opening lower and continuing the move. Then it started back up and moved into plus territory, then dropped off, closing 5 points in loss territory.

In theory you could have gained in both directions, but it never works that way. Indeed, days like this are invitations to lose in both directions. It's like a boxer falling for a feint and then getting knocked out. You see the market starting out on a strong move, in this case it was down and the temptation to sell short is strong. But look at the overall picture. The market was in a stabilizing episode, after huge swings upward from 1900 to over 2400, and then into a 200 point correction. If reason plays any role in such matters, it would have seemed prudent for all market hands to stand back and take a deep breath or two, after such movement. So, only a very fast track operator would have been seduced into the futures market on that day, April 23. By the time you had decided to sell short, the chances are the move had already eaten up much of its destination, so that you would have been caught on the wrong side—unless you are a born financial commodities trader who can sniff right moves from wrong. Such people exist but they don't read books, they play the markets.

The end of April saw no clarification or the establishment of a trend. The correction, from above 2420 down to 2180 (intraday) appeared to have run its course. Now we were in combination territory, not stock index futures country. May 5 produced a big jump in the Dow and the OEX but only a modest move in the index futures. This sometimes happens, admittedly not often. It was the first day of the period we're watching that the use of the index future would have made any sense. But you would have had to get in early and hold on through the course of the day.

A single robin is not evidence for spring, nor is a single S&P up day a sign of a roaring bull. Consider that on May 5 the Dow rose almost 52 points on sharply increased volume from the day before, and utilities and transportation indexes also advanced. If you look at the trading throughout the day, it was not conducive to aspirin-free futures contracts, yet that is what we seek. The Dow opened at 2303, went up to 2306, then to 2312, 2317, 2330 and thence its final up movement. A perfect day, you say, but the S&P index started on the upswing, then turned around and dropped a full point. Thereupon it righted itself and performed in tandem with the rest of the market. A 12 tick stop-loss order would have washed you out of the 25 tick down move, but would you have had the gumption to rush back in for what then became an easy roll to well over $2,000 for the day? That is a personal as well as a market question. Yet May 5 was the first day to meet our specifications (above) for trading.

There are days such as May 11, 1987, when the market commenced the right behavior for our purposes, with virtually all the bells ringing, the flags waving, and then took it all back. It shot up over 30 points early on, held most of the gains for much of the day, on good volume, but closed down 15 points. The S&P index gained over 4 points, but lost 3 1/2 on the day. If you had plunged in at the opening signals, would you have been wise enough to take your gains at 2 or 3 1/2 points? If not, you would have been a candidate for a sharp loss on the day. Such days are what make this contract both hair-raising and hair-tearing. May 12 (next day) was an inversion of May 11. The market fell at the beginning and rose at the end, finishing up the 15 points it had lost the day before. Yet the S&P index marked time, finishing up a mere .30. But during the day it dropped almost 4 points, or $2,000 worth. Retrospectively it is clear that this market was not for our trading purposes, but perfect for the combination selling we were doing. That is the psychological and technical reason why I keep insisting on diversity of speculative efforts. It's your private conglomeration, in which you control a glue factory as well as a horse grooming stable. When the horses are in no need of attention it may be time to stir the glue pots. You can't just sit there. The problem of retrospection—only learning all there is to know after the fact—is the age-old view that history has something to teach us. It does indeed, but the larger question of whether we can learn from history is an individual matter. Napoleon lacked a recent professor of Russian campaigns to help him avoid catastrophe, but what excuse did the Kaiser and Hitler have?

In the first two weeks of May 1987, the Dow was trading between 2180 and 2380. These were rarefied heights. Most of us were used to a Dow trading below 1000 all our lives when a swing of 50 or 75 points was eyebrow raising, a swing of 100 was a major market trend, and the usual daily movement was rarely more than 10 points. The higher the Dow the dizzier the swings, but not the percentage of swings, necessarily. The market isn't much more volatile, and some studies show that other periods have had similar or greater volatilities. The high numbers create an illusion. The computer and program trading, and the much higher volume, have certainly compressed market events in time. That affects the individual investor, whose psychology may not be geared to the emotional demands created by all the razzle dazzle. Therein lies the problem; the market is indifferent to the investor but the converse is not true.

On Friday, May 15, the market took a sharp nosedive, losing 53 points. The S&P futures index dropped over 7 points. During much of the day the market was up. The nosedive started after noon. A day trader, following every tick, might have been tempted into such a market, and if he had the direction right and sold short, he would have made several thousand dollars per contract. But again, the right bells were not ringing—the major signs we've enumerated; advance/decline ratios, the TRIN, market breadth, and so on. They rang sporadically, as they always do in such a situation. Overall, in the context of the broad market drama, and looking back to the January to April drive from 1900 to 2400, we could not discern a new trend, once the market reached the 2400 level. Ultimately, that is our final criterion, based on the indicators (and market timing services) we follow, as they are consistent with our general market-economic approach.

Throughout the remainder of May the market chugged back from some of its April correction, but not enough to start a new trend. A day trader might have entered the market May

26, when it had a big leap of 55 points, and the S&P index jumped almost 8, which is almost $4,000 per contract, and not a bad day's work. Indeed, that was the only other day of the entire period under review that our system was giving us some strong encouragement. The market, however, was not all a rosy scenario; it fell off in the morning, before making its move—a not unfamiliar stance. We prefer to enter a market in which there are few or no ambiguities through the list of signals we keep. It doesn't happen often—three to five times a year—but when it does you can usually bank on it, literally.

C H A P T E R 8

Conclusion

OEX options, as traded in this book, are speculative but mostly of low risk. The use of the vertical spread in Strategy One assures a skilled trader of better than even odds that profits are possible.

In my first options book, *Taking Profits From The OEX,* I suggested that selling both sides of combinations would be the royal road to riches. But that was before the events of October 1987 and October 1989—the two biggest market traumas. If such events are destined to occur every two years, even if they continue to happen exclusively in October—a hardly likely scenario—it becomes necessary to take counter measures. Much of this book consists of that philosophy.

As we've stressed, the vertical spread is the OEX trader's answer to market crises brought on by computerized trading. Before the 1987 crash an OEX trader could adjust to most market ups and downs with quick action and strategy adjustment. That no longer works. Selling combinations turned out to be excessively risky no matter what adjustments could be made.

In the new market atmosphere, in which almost a million OEX participants continue to challenge the beast, a new strategic concept needed to be articulated. That is the reason for this book. For even if vertical spread tactics are slightly more complicated than simple combination selling or spreading (or buying), they are easily learned with not much more effort than any other option strategy. They are far less risky and ultimately no less profitable once mastered.

The vertical spread (Strategy One) is not of course the only answer to the new volatility of markets and the OEX. It is the base of a new attitude towards risk control using other instruments in tandem. These include bull and bear spreads and options buying.

Of the near-one-million daily OEX players, options buying is the primary or only strategy. You risk the total of what you buy but no more. In trending markets one can hardly do better with the OEX. But most markets do not trend; they yawn. That is where vertical spreads become your friend. No trend turns out to be your best friend.

One could enumerate goals of buying OEX options as portfolio insurance or the various uses of options other than OEX in hedging strategies, such as buying a stock and selling a covered option on it—the "buy-write" strategy. All have their uses but they belong to another book, another attitude.

Four years later the S&P 500 picture has changed to this extent. There is now an S&P index, like the OEX index. Instead of being based on the 100 largest stocks, it is based on the S&P 500 largest stocks. So, it more closely and narrowly follows the general market. Moreover, it works more or less exactly like the OEX, with strike prices at 5-point intervals, and with three month expiration periods. You can use the same strategies on it as on the OEX. Is it an exact duplication? No, but close enough to warrant interest. You can use the same strategies that apply to the OEX, but anything based on the S&P 500 will be highly volatile, so expect a somewhat rougher ride than you get on the OEX. The S&P 500 moves through a wider range of strike prices on a typical day, but usually parallels the OEX in gains or losses each day. It moves more rapidly during the day, as it must if it is to travel greater distances. So it is scarier. That's because it's based on a financial futures index and like any other futures index (e.g., cattle) it has high volatility.

Glossary

ARBITRAGE.

Simultaneous purchase and sale of similar financial instruments in hopes of making a profit from an expected change of price relationship.

AT-THE-MONEY.

An option whose strike price is the same as the OEX index. With the OEX at 290, the 290 options are at-the-money. The condition is fleeting; these options take on the performance of what they turn into immediately—in-the-money or out-of-the-money options.

BEAR SPREAD.

A spread undertaken in the belief that the market is declining. You buy an in-the-money OEX put with the strike price closest to the current OEX index, and you sell the out-of-the-money put with the strike price closest to the same index level. Both options have the same expiration date. In a bear *time* spread you use different expiration months, buying the more distant option and selling the nearby option with the same exercise (strike) price. One should never pay more than 2 1/2 ($250) per contract for a spread.

BULL SPREAD.

Converse of bear spread. A spread entered into in the belief that the market is advancing and will continue to do so long enough to allow the spread to widen to an optimum of the $5 difference between the OEX option you buy and the one you sell. You always buy an in-the-money call with the strike price closest to the index, and you sell the out-of-the-money option with the strike price closest to the same index. Both options should have the same expiration date. You should not pay more than 2 1/2, ($250) per contract, as with bear spreads.

BUYING SPREADS.

In contrast with selling spreads, in which you post a margin, when you buy spreads no margin is required. That's because you make a payment when you buy the more expensive option while you sell the less expensive one, which is the procedure when you put on a spread.

CALENDAR SPREAD.

A spread with the same exercise price for both put and call members, but with different expiration dates. Also called a time or horizontal spread.

CLOSING TRANSACTION.

Closing out a position. Buying back the option you sold; selling the option you bought.

CREDIT.

A positive balance.

CYCLES.

Cycles and cycle theories are among the oldest in market history. The most famous is the Kondratieff Wave cycle of fifty years, formulated by a Russian economist in Stalin's time. Stalin had him murdered because he was not a Marxist. His theory was that capitalism moved in fifty-year waves of expansion and contraction. Cycles of hours, days, weeks, months and years, are traced by modern market theorists, some of whom can point to outstanding successes in calling market turns.

DEBIT.

A negative balance.

EXERCISE PRICES.

OEX (and other option) prices are set at five point intervals bracketed around the current index value. New exercise prices are added when the index goes up or down to the limits of the existing strike prices. Limits are dictated by market movements. When the market exceeds highest or lowest exercise prices, new ones are added.

EXPIRATION DATE.

The S&P 100 index options (OEX) expire each month on the third Friday (actually on Saturday, for bookkeeping).

FLOOR BROKER.

A broker who executes customer orders. Must be licensed by the CFTC (Commodity Futures Trading Commission).

FLOOR TRADER.

One who trades only for his or her own account. Also known as a "local."

IN-THE-MONEY.

Also, intrinsic value. When the price of the daily OEX index is higher than the strike price of the call or lower than the price of the put.

INTRINSIC VALUE.

The amount of value in an option above and beyond time value. Also, real value. It's the difference between the strike price and the index price when, in the case of a call, the index is above the strike price. Thus, with the OEX index at 286 a Jun call having intrinsic value was 280, on May 28, 1987, at 9 3/4, or $975.00. Note that the Jul 280 calls were 12 3/4, indicating that the market awarded 3 points extra for the additional time. So the Jul 280 had 9 3/4 intrinsic value and 3 points of time value. On the put side, with the index at 286, the 290 Jun put had 7 1/4 intrinsic value, the 290 Jul puts were at

10, or 2 3/4 time value in addition to the 7 1/4. It may be argued that these value designations are inexact. Thus the 9 3/4 price on the Jun 286 call was not entirely intrinsic value, but also contained some time value. But there is no breakdown each day of time versus intrinsic value. It isn't until the cycle nears its end, when the far out-of-the-money strike prices are at 1/16 that intrinsic value becomes crystal clear.

LIMIT ORDER.
A customer order to a broker that specifies a price.

MARGIN.
The amount of money you deposit with your broker that qualifies you to trade OEX combinations. It can also be stock or bond certificates. The amount depends on where the OEX index is—the higher the index the higher the margin, allowing for some variation between brokerage houses. With the OEX around 300 each contract requires about $1,000 in margin. Margin requirement goes up and down with the OEX index. Margin costs, generally, have increased sharply since the events of October 1987 and October 1989.

MARGIN CALL.
Demand for additional margin money when the market goes against your position. A school of thought argues that one should never pay a margin call, but instead should get out of the contract, taking the loss, and undertake a more favorable position. Needless to say, another school of thought disputes this view on the assumption that market wisdom should be your guide. If you have reason to believe that the unfavorable market move may be corrected without further loss, it could well be to your advantage to pay the margin call. Since paying a margin call is about as pleasant as drinking hemlock, without thereby achieving immortality, each person must decide what course to take. When you pay a margin call you have not taken corrective action, instead you are waiting for the market to take corrective

action, which it may disdain to do. What corrective action can be taken? If the margin call is against the call side of a combination, you can buy back the losing call, usually at from $750 to $1000 per contract, some of which will be offset by gains on the put side, and wait for the market to settle down, if indeed it does. You then sell a new call that may well restore the original position, recouping part and in some cases all of your loss.

OUT-OF-THE-MONEY.

When the price of the OEX index is above the strike price of the call, and when the price of the OEX index is below the strike price of the put. With the OEX index at 286, these Jun call strike prices are out-of-the-money: 290 at 4 1/8; 295 at 2 3/8; 300 at 1 1/4; 305 at 9/16 and 310 at 3/16. Clearly the closer you get to an in-the-money status, or at-the-money, the higher the price the market places on the option.

PREMIUMS.

Option premiums or values are expressed in points and fractions. Each point equals $100. The minimum fraction is 1/16 for options trading below 3, and 1/8 for all others. A premium of 1 1/16 equals $106.25.

PUBLIC LIMIT ORDER BOOK.

An important aspect of OEX trading, this book enables a public customer to place a limit order and have it executed by an official of the Order Book. Exchange employees are book officials. They accept only public orders and are required to execute these orders on the book before accepting orders from the floor at the same or higher prices.

STRIKE PRICES.

Same as exercise prices.

TIME VALUE.

Value given by the market to an unexpired option, above and beyond its intrinsic or real value. For example: with the

OEX index at 286, a Jun 285 call, about three weeks from expiration, has a premium of 6 5/8. How much is time value and how much is intrinsic value? By the standard formulation of value, intrinsic value is the amount the option is in-the-money. In that case this option has only 1 point of intrinsic value and 5 5/8 points of time value. But the Jun 280 OEX call has 9 3/4 points of premium, which should give it 6 points of real or intrinsic value and 3 3/4 points of time value. So there is a discrepancy here; why should options separated by 5 points of strike price have so much disparity in their time values, seeing that the one has 5 5/8, the other 3 3/4 points of time value? Presumably the market is saying that the option with the higher amount of time value is riskier, and markets always pay higher values on risk.

Index